## CORE SKILLS

**GRADE 4**

# Test Preparation

**Strategies for**
- *Reading*
- *Vocabulary*
- *Math*
- *Listening*
- *Language*

## STECK-VAUGHN
ELEMENTARY · SECONDARY · ADULT · LIBRARY

A Harcourt Company

www.svschoolsupply.com

# Core Skills: Test Preparation
## Grade 4

# Contents

ISBN 0-7398-5737-1

2 3 4 5 6 7 8 9   DBH   06 05 04 03 02

Dear Parent,

Welcome to *Steck-Vaughn Core Skills: Test Preparation*. You have selected a book that will help your child develop the skills he or she needs to succeed on standardized tests.

Although testing can be a source of anxiety for children, this book will give your child the preparation and practice that he or she needs to feel better prepared and more confident when taking a standardized test. Research shows that children who are acquainted with the scoring format of standardized tests score higher on those tests. Students also score higher when they practice and understand the skills and strategies needed to take standardized tests. The subject areas and concepts presented in this book are typically found on standardized tests at this grade level.

To best help your child, please consider the following suggestions:

- Provide a quiet place to work.
- Go over the directions and the sample exercises together.
- Review the strategy tips.
- Reassure your child that the practice tests are not "real" tests.
- Encourage your child to do his or her best.
- Check the lesson when it is complete.
- Go over the answers and note improvements as well as problems.

If your child expresses anxiety about taking a test or completing these lessons, help him or her understand what causes the stress. Then, talk about ways to eliminate anxiety. Above all, enjoy this time you spend with your child. He or she will feel your support, and test scores will improve as success in test taking is experienced.

Help your child maintain a positive attitude about taking a standardized test. Let your child know that each test provides an opportunity to shine.

Sincerely,

The Educators and Staff of
Steck-Vaughn School Supply

P.S. You might want to visit our website at **www.svschoolsupply.com** for more test preparation materials as well as additional review of content areas.

Dear Student,

Sometime during the school year, you will be taking standardized tests. This book can help you prepare to take such tests.

Here are some suggestions for using these practice tests and for taking the "real" tests.

**DO:**
- Listen to or read all the directions.
- Read the **Try This** strategy tips, do the **Sample** items, and then look at **Think It Through** to check your answer before you begin each lesson.
- Look over the entire test or section before you begin.
- Stay calm, concentrate on the test, and clear your mind of things that have nothing to do with the test.
- Read all the answer choices before choosing the one that you think is best.
- Make sure the number you fill in on the answer sheet matches the question number on the test page.
- Trust your first instinct when answering each question.
- Answer the easy questions first, then go back and work on the ones you aren't sure about.
- Take all the time you are allowed.

**DON'T:**
- Look ahead to another question until you complete the one you're working on.
- Spend too much time on one question.
- Rush.
- Worry if others finish while you are still working.
- Change an answer unless you are really sure it should be changed.

**Remember to do your best!**

# Core Skills: Test Preparation

## Introduction

Standardized tests are becoming increasingly more important in both public and private schools, yet test anxiety causes many children to perform below their fullest potential.
*Core Skills: Test Preparation* is designed to help children succeed on standardized tests. This program refreshes basic skills, familiarizes children with test formats and directions, and teaches test-taking strategies.

A large part of being well prepared for a test is knowing how to approach different types of questions and learning how to use time wisely. *Core Skills: Test Preparation* gives children the opportunity to take a test under conditions that parallel those they will face when taking standardized tests. This practice and experience will allow them to feel more confident when taking standardized tests and will enable them to demonstrate their knowledge successfully.

## Tools for Success

*Core Skills: Test Preparation* gives children valuable practice with the content areas and question formats of the major standardized tests used nationally. These include:

- CAT (California Achievement Tests)
- CTBS (Comprehensive Tests of Basic Skills)
- ITBS (Iowa Tests of Basic Skills)
- MAT (Metropolitan Achievement Tests)
- SAT (Stanford Achievement Test)

*Core Skills: Test Preparation* provides:

- Test-taking strategies
- Familiarity with test directions
- Review of skills and content
- Awareness of test formats
- Practice tests

## Organization

The book is divided into units that correspond to those found on standardized tests. These include:

- Reading Comprehension
- Reading Vocabulary
- Mathematics Problem Solving and Procedures
- Listening
- Language

Each skill lesson includes:

**Directions**—clear, concise, and similar to those found on standardized tests;

**Try This**—a skill strategy that enables children to approach each lesson exercise in a logical way;

A **Sample**—to familiarize children with test-taking items;

**Think It Through**—a specific explanation of the correct answer in the sample item; and

A **Practice Section**—a set of exercises based on the lesson and modeled on the kinds of exercises found on standardized tests.

Each unit is followed by a **Unit Test** that covers all of the skills in the unit and allows children the opportunity to experience a situation similar to the testing situation. The book concludes with five **Practice Tests** that correspond to the content areas covered in the lessons. Two sets of **Answer Sheets** are provided for the Practice Tests answers.

## Icons

 A script that must be read aloud accompanies each listening skill lesson or test. These types of activities are denoted with an icon to let you and your child know that it is time to work together.

 The **Practice Tests** are timed tests and the stopwatch icon indicates the amount of time allotted for each test.

*Core Skills: Test Preparation* lessons and practice provide children with the tools they need to build their self-confidence. That self-confidence can translate into a positive test-taking experience and higher scores on standardized tests. With its emphasis on skills, strategies for success, and practice, *Core Skills: Test Preparation* gives children the ability to succeed on standardized tests.

# Standardized Test Content Areas

## Reading Skills

Identifying synonyms

Using sentence context to determine word meaning of multiple-meaning words

Using sentence context to determine word meaning

Interpreting the main idea

Recalling specific details

Making inferences

Drawing conclusions

Extending meaning

Using context to determine word meaning

Identifying actions, reasons, and sequence

Understanding cause and effect

Predicting outcomes

Using definitional phrases to determine word meanings

## Language Skills

Determining topic relevance

Organizing information

Identifying the correct use of general reference materials

Interpreting dictionary entries

Determining correct alphabetical order of words beginning with different letters

Using a table of contents and an index of a book to locate information

Identifying clearly written sentences

Determining appropriate topic sentences and supporting sentences

Identifying extraneous information within a paragraph

Identifying correctly applied grammar

Identifying correct capitalization and punctuation

Recognizing misspelled words in context

Identifying correct spellings of words in context

## Mathematics Skills

Identifying odd and even numbers

Understanding expanded notation

Understanding place value

Comparing and ordering whole numbers, fractions, and decimals

Understanding inverse operations

Identifying fractional parts and understanding decimals

Reading and interpreting bar graphs, tables, and tally charts

Identifying and predicting outcomes and determining simple probability

Identifying plane figures, components of geometric figures, symmetry, rotations, and reflections

Classifying and comparing angles

Counting and trading coins and bills

Identifying correct change

Comparing lengths and areas

Selecting appropriate units of measurement and estimating using customary and metric units

Identifying elapsed time

Estimating temperatures

Reading scales of length, temperature, weight, or capacity

Completing number and geometric patterns

Using estimation in problem solving

Identifying reasonableness

Identifying the operations needed to solve problems

Identifying missing information

Demonstrating the ability to add, subtract, multiply, and divide

Rounding

Applying the concepts of addition, subtraction, multiplication, and division to word problems

# Listening Scripts

These scripts accompany the listening portions of the lessons and tests found in Unit 7 on pages 77–80 and in Unit 12 on pages 117 and 118. For the lessons in Unit 7, read the directions and the **Try This** strategy to your child before doing the sample question. After completing the sample question, go over the correct answer using **Think It Through**. Then begin the lesson. In the Unit 7 and 12 tests, do the sample question at the top of the page before beginning the test. In all listening lessons and tests, give your child time to respond before reading the next question. You may read these items twice if needed.

## Unit 7: Listening

### Listening for Word Meanings, p. 77

**Reading Skill:** Using definitional phrases to determine word meaning

Look at Sample A. I will read a sentence and four answer choices. You will find the word that best completes the sentence. Listen carefully. If something is amusing, it is—A difficult ... B polished ... C funny ... D frightening.

Now you will practice finding more words that best complete sentences. We will do numbers 1 through 10. Listen carefully to the sentence and the four answer choices. Then darken the circle for the correct answer.

1  To decrease means to—A make smaller ...
   B make larger ... C make better ...
   D make worse.
2  A region is—F a plan ... G a ruler ...
   H an area ... J a village.
3  A cabin is a kind of—A house ... B car ...
   C dance ... D boat.
4  A duet is a kind of—F song for two ...
   G carnival for many ... H role for a child ...
   J game for three.
5  If something is fancy, it is—A real ...
   B valuable ... C false ... D decorated.
6  A banquet is a kind of—F feast ... G meeting ...
   H concert ... J wedding.
7  To avoid something is to—A dodge it ...
   B welcome it ... C think about it ...
   D reward it.
8  If performers are talented, they are—
   F ordinary ... G familiar ... H skillful ...
   J elementary.
9  If you accept something, you—A receive it ...
   B sell it ... C clean it ... D trade it.
10 A scheme is a kind of—F story ...
   G place ... H person ... J plan.

### Building Listening Skills, p. 78

**Reading Skill:** Recalling specific details; understanding actions, reasons, and sequence; making inferences; extending meaning

Look at Sample A. I will read a story and then ask a question. You will choose the best answer to the question. Listen carefully. Spiders use their silk thread to spin webs. The thread comes from inside their bodies. Then they use their webs to catch their prey. What do spiders spin their webs from?
A grass ... B cotton ... C silk ... D wool.

Now you will practice choosing more words and phrases that best answer questions about stories that you hear. We will do numbers 1 through 12. Listen to the story and the questions. Then darken the circle for the correct answer.

Listen to this story. You will answer two questions.

> Mammoths were very large creatures. They lived eleven thousand years ago. Mammoths looked like elephants. We know that they looked like elephants because some mammoths were preserved in ice when they died.

1  Which word best describes mammoths?
   A huge ... B warm ... C friendly ... D small.
2  Mammoths looked like—F whales ...
   G horses ... H dinosaurs ... J elephants.

Now find number 3. Listen to this paragraph. You will answer two questions.

> Samantha's cat had three kittens. Samantha knew that she would not be able to keep them, so she posted a sign in the grocery store. The sign described the kittens. Samantha soon found good homes for all of her kittens.

3  Samantha posted a sign in—A the mall ...
   B the grocery store ... C her school ...
   D the library.
4  How many kittens did Samantha's cat have?
   F six ... G two ... H three ... J four.

Now find number 5. Listen to this commercial. You will answer five questions.

Do you have trouble misplacing your pencils while you are working? Try our amazing Stick-To-You pencil. This is a high-quality No. 2 pencil, the kind preferred by 9 out of 10 teachers. What makes it special is how easy it is to keep track of. Just peel off the special adhesive backing. It automatically sticks to any surface, time and time again. You can keep your pencil on a desk or table, or even on your clothes! Never lose your pencil again. Buy the Stick-To-You pencil for a fabulously low price. Find the Stick-To-You pencil at fine grocery stores near you. You'll love it!

5  The purpose of this advertisement is to—
   A complain about lost pencils ... B get you to go to a grocery store ... C sell you a product ...
   D tell how pencils are made.
6  Which of these is a fact about the Stick-To-You pencil?
   F It is a No. 2 pencil. ... G It is easy to keep track of. ... H You'll love it. ... J It is special.
7  According to the commercial, where can you buy the Stick-To-You pencil? A at a grocery store ...
   B at a hardware store ... C at a pet store ...
   D at a convenience store.
8  How is the Stick-To-You pencil different from other pencils? F You can buy it at a grocery store. ...
   G It is a No. 2 pencil. ... H It is easier to write with. ... J It has an adhesive backing.
9  How many teachers prefer a number two pencil?
   A 8 out of 10 ... B 5 out of 10 ...
   C 9 out of 10 ... D 10 out of 10.

Now find number 10. Listen to these directions. You will answer three questions.

To get from the entrance of City Park to the picnic area, follow the road north. You will pass the soccer fields. Just after you pass the soccer fields, turn right. You can park in any of the spaces by the playground. You will see the picnic tables under the trees. Behind the trees is Metro Creek.

10  What is located behind the picnic area?
   F Metro Creek ... G soccer fields ...
   H the exit ... J the playground.
11  Which of the following is not mentioned in the directions? A a picnic area ...
   B a playground ... C tennis courts ...
   D soccer fields.
12  What do these directions tell? F how to get to City Park from downtown ... G how to get from the entrance of City Park to the picnic area ...
   H how to get to the local lake ...
   J how to get to the new golf course.

## Test, pp. 79–80

In this test you will use the listening skills we have practiced in this unit. This test is divided into two parts. For each part there is a sample exercise. Look at Sample A. In this part of the test, you will choose words or groups of words that best complete sentences. I will read part of a sentence and four answer choices. Listen carefully. The lobby of a building is its—
A address ... B dining hall ... C entrance hall ... D kitchen.  Darken the circle for the word that means the same as lobby.

You should have darkened C, entrance hall, because lobby means the same as entrance hall.

Now you will choose more words that best complete sentences. We will do numbers 1 through 13. Listen carefully to the sentence and the four answer choices. Then darken the circle for the correct answer.

1  To astonish is to—A amaze ... B receive ...
   C work ... D push.
2  To capture is to—F give away ... G stumble over ... H take by force ... J find out.
3  If something is risky, it is—A new ... B easy ...
   C dangerous ... D childish.
4  To terrify is to—F surprise … G remember …
   H frighten … J forget.
5  A grove is a group of—A trees … B animals …
   C people … D flowers.
6  To mumble is to speak—F loudly ...
   G unclearly ... H slowly ... J quickly.
7  Beneath means A again ... B under ...
   C hardly ... D almost.
8  A morsel is a—F small bite ... G fresh piece ...
   H large slice ... J spoiled part.
9  Something that is slippery is—A shiny …
   B slick … C soft … D small.
10  If you are fond of something, you—F sell it ...
   G like it ... H hide it ... J lose it.
11  The core of an object is its—A crust ...
   B center ... C size ... D color.
12  To propose something is to—F suggest it ...
   G write it ... H show it ... J bury it.
13  If you are weary, you are—A tired ...
   B foolish ... C clever ... D guilty.

Now turn to page 80.

Look at Sample B. In this part of the test, you will choose words or groups of words that best answer questions about paragraphs and stories that you hear. I will read a story and then ask a question. You will choose the best answer to the question. Listen carefully. Sandra knew what she wanted to buy her mom for Mother's Day. She had seen a dress in the dress shop window. She saved twenty dollars to buy the dress. Later, when she went to buy the dress, she was disappointed to find out that the dress cost one hundred dollars. How much money did the dress cost? A two hundred dollars ... B twenty dollars ... C one hundred dollars ... D fifty dollars.

You should have darkened C, one hundred dollars, because the last sentence of the story says that Sandra found out that the dress cost one hundred dollars.

Now you will choose more words or groups of words that best answer questions. We will do numbers 14 through 25. Listen carefully to the story and question. Then darken the circle for the correct answer.

Listen to these rules. You will answer three questions.

All swimmers at Greenwood Community Swimming Pool must follow these rules:

1. No running in the pool area.
2. No glass containers in the pool area.
3. No food or drinks in the pool.
4. No pets in or around the pool.
5. No splashing or rowdy behavior in the pool.

14 These rules are probably posted to—F keep people from using the pool ... G keep people safe at the pool ... H keep people from having fun at the pool ... J keep the pool from getting crowded.
15 Which of the following is not allowed? A Talking … B Running … C Diving … D Laughing.
16 What is not allowed in the pool area? F Glass containers ... G Children ... H Picnic baskets ... J Plastic containers.

Now find number 17. Listen to this story. You will answer four questions.

It was a cold, snowy day. When Josh came home from school, he went outside and built a snowman. He dressed the snowman up with buttons, a scarf, and a pair of sunglasses. In school the next day, Josh thought about his snowman. Jeff could hardly wait for school to end so he could go home and see it. The sun was out. Spring was on the way. When he got home, Josh ran into the back yard to see his snowman. He couldn't believe what he saw.

17 The snowman was wearing all of the following except—A sunglasses ... B buttons ... C a scarf ... D a hat.
18 When he went into the back yard, Josh probably felt—F happy ... G curious ... H excited ... J sad.
19 Josh's snowman probably—A grew ... B melted ... C talked ... D fell.
20 A good title for this story is—F "A Winter Day" ... G "How to Make a Snowman" ... H "Spring Is Coming" ... J "Josh and His Snowman".

Now find number 21. Listen to this story. You will answer five questions.

Hurricanes are dangerous storms that occur in some parts of the United States. They often occur in states near the Atlantic Ocean or the Gulf of Mexico. Hurricanes develop over warm ocean water, but then they can move over land. They bring heavy rain and strong winds. To be called a hurricane, a storm must have winds of at least 75 miles an hour. The hurricane season in the United States is from June to November each year.

21 Hurricane season in the United States is during the—A summer and fall ... B spring and summer ... C fall and winter ... D winter and spring.
22 A hurricane has winds of at least—F 35 miles an hour ... G 50 miles an hour ... H 75 miles an hour ... J 100 miles an hour.
23 In the United States, hurricanes occur in— A states along the Great Lakes ... B states along the Mississippi River ... C states along the Atlantic Ocean ... D all states.
24 Hurricanes develop over—F cool ocean water ... G warm ocean water … H cool land … J warm land.
25 The purpose of this paragraph is to—A tell a story about hurricanes ... B describe famous hurricanes ... C give information about hurricanes ... D teach hurricane safety.

# Unit 12: Comprehensive Test

## Practice Test 4:
## Listening, pp. 117–118

(Give your child scratch paper to take notes if needed.)

In this test you will use your listening skills to answer questions. This test is divided into two parts. For each part there is a sample exercise. Look at Sample A. In this part of the test, you will choose the words that best complete sentences. I will read a sentence and the four answer choices. You will find the word or group of words that best completes the sentence. Listen carefully. Something that is a fluid is—A liquid … B solid … C hard … D sticky. Darken the circle for the word that best completes the sentence.

You should have darkened the circle for A, liquid, because fluid means liquid.

Now you will choose more words that best complete sentences. We will do numbers 1 through 13. Listen carefully to the sentence and the four answer choices. Then darken the circle for the correct answer.

1   If something is abrupt it is—A sudden …
    B gradual … C accidental … D tearful.
2   To chart something is to—F make a map of …
    G march toward … H escape to …
    J settle along.
3   To be keen about something is to be—
    A confused … B eager …  C rich … D lazy.
4   To sway is to—F announce … G swing …
    H shrink … J break off.
5   To flatter someone is to—A give advice …
    B find a mistake … C offer to help …
    D praise too much.
6   Mournful means—F soft … G sad …
    H skillful … J surprising.
7   Someone who is cautious is—A lying …
    B careful … C daring … D bored.
8   If something is peculiar it is—F normal …
    G ordinary … H grateful … J strange.
9   To complain is to—A praise … B laugh aloud …
    C find fault … D leave.
10  To pose is to—F send … G shower …
    H estimate … J model.
11  Someone who is faithful is—A silly …
    B mean … C loyal … D sneaky.
12  To lack is to—F be without … G build up …
    H gain … J use.
13  An uproar is a—A loud noise … B thought …
    C calmness … D serious problem.

Now turn to page 118.

Look at Sample B. In this part of the test, you will choose the words or groups of words that best answer questions about paragraphs and stories that you hear. I will read a story and then ask a question. You will choose the best answer to the question. Listen carefully. Fran loves playing on the beach and building things with sand. She has made castles, skyscrapers, flying saucers, and animals. Fran would like to become a famous artist and sculptor someday. "Sand art is lots of fun, but the tide washes it away," says Fran. She wants to make art that will last forever. You can tell from the story that Fran likes—
A to read … B to go to the beach … C to study famous people … D to go to school. Darken the circle for the correct answer.

You should have darkened the circle for B, to go to the beach, because the story says that Fran loves playing on the beach and building things with sand.

Now you will choose more words or groups of words that best answer questions about paragraphs and stories that you hear. We will do numbers 14 through 25. Listen carefully to the story and the question. Then darken the circle for the correct answer.

Listen as I read this story. You will answer three questions.

> "Jeff, you'll really enjoy reading *Pinocchio*. It's a story about the adventures of a wooden puppet that comes to life. I loved the story. When you finish the book, let's go to the library and check out some more books to read."

14  After Jeff finishes *Pinocchio*, he will probably go to the—F library … G mall … H store … J park.
15  *Pinocchio* is about—A a dog … B a princess …
    C a puppet … D a wizard.
16  This passage is most like—F a conversation …
    G a newspaper article … H a letter …  J a story.

Now find number 17. Listen to this commercial. You will answer three questions.

Enjoy family fun at the Fun Station. The Fun Station offers every kind of excitement any family could want. There are bumper cars, boat rides, miniature golf, an arcade, a carousel, and more. After being entertained, enjoy delicious food at our Food Bazaar. All of this is available at a tremendous discount off the entrance fee for your group of four or more. Come to the Fun Station for a "funtastic" time! There is no better place for your family's entertainment.

17   Which of these is not mentioned in the commercial? A movies … B bumper cars … C boat rides … D miniature golf.
18   How can you get a discount off the entrance fee? F mention the ad … G bring a group of four or more … H bring a coupon … J ask the manager.

Now find number 19. Listen carefully as I read these directions. You will answer three questions.

Here's how to make a fun, easy treat. Peel a banana and cut it into fourths. Insert a round toothpick into each fourth. Then dip the banana pieces into honey. Next, roll each piece in coconut. Last, put the pieces in the freezer. After several hours, you'll have a tasty frozen snack.

19   What do these directions tell how to do? A make gingerbread … B make a frozen banana treat … C make cookies … D make an ice cream sundae.
20   What do the directions say to do after dipping the banana in honey? F peel the banana … G put the banana in the freezer … H dip the banana in honey again … J roll the banana in coconut.

Now find number 21. Listen to this note. You will answer five questions.

George, Lee, and Mica volunteer at the community center every Saturday afternoon. One Saturday they saw a note from Mrs. Allen, the director of the community center. The note was on the bulletin board, and this is what it said:

Lee: Could you help Mr. Yasuda? He is teaching a pottery class today. He will need help setting up before the class. He will also need help cleaning up after the class. While the class is going on, you can work with the kids in the class.

George: The Spring Community Fiesta is tonight. Ms. Dole needs your help decorating the gym.

Mica: Please help Mr. Weiss today. He is planting a vegetable garden in back of the community center.

21   The purpose of the note is to—A list the various activities offered at the community center … B give instructions to the center volunteers … C advertise the events held at the community center … D list the teachers and classes offered at the community center.
22   The community center is getting ready for a— F garden show … G gymnastics competition … H fall banquet … J spring fiesta.
23   Mica is going to help—A Mr. Weiss … B Ms. Dole … C Mr. Yasuda … D Mrs. Allen.
24   Mr. Yasuda is teaching—F a gardening class … G a pottery class … H a cake decorating class … J an exercise class.
25   Mrs. Allen is—A decorating the gym … B planting a vegetable garden … C the community center's director … D the pottery teacher.

The following strategies will help you do your best on standardized reading tests. These three strategies will assist you in organizing the information needed to successfully answer the questions.

## STRATEGY 1

### The CHECK AND SEE Strategy
This strategy can be used when a question asks for a fact from the story. The answer to the question is right there in the story. It is not hidden. Some of the same words may be in the story and in the question.

 **Check and See** will help you answer *remembering information* questions.

### This is the Check and See Strategy

1. **READ: Read** the question.

2. **FIND: Find** the words you need in the story.

3. **DECIDE: Decide** which strategy to use.
   **Check and See:** Put a **check** next to the sentence where you can **see** the words you need to answer the question.

4. **ANSWER:** Choose the best **answer**.

GO ON

## STRATEGY 2

### The PUZZLE PIECE Strategy

This strategy can be used when a question asks you what something means. Sometimes there does not seem to be an answer. It is not stated in the story.

**Puzzle Piece** is the strategy to use when you must fit facts together to get the answer. This is like putting a puzzle together. Puzzles are made up of many pieces. You cannot look at one piece and know what the picture is. Only when you put the pieces together can you see the whole picture.

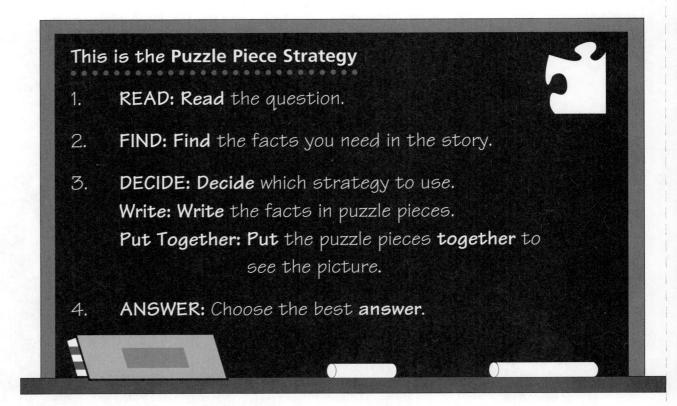

**This is the Puzzle Piece Strategy**

1.  READ: **Read** the question.

2.  FIND: **Find** the facts you need in the story.

3.  DECIDE: **Decide** which strategy to use.
    Write: **Write** the facts in puzzle pieces.
    Put Together: **Put** the puzzle pieces **together** to see the picture.

4.  ANSWER: Choose the best **answer**.

GO ON

## STRATEGY 3

### The WHAT LIGHTS UP Strategy

This is another strategy you can use when an answer is not in the story. To answer the question you need to add your own ideas to the story. This added information can come from your own experiences.

 **What Lights Up** can help you see if something is true, real, useful, or a fact. It can help you see what would happen if the story had a different ending.

You can use the **What Lights Up Strategy** to answer the hardest type of question. This is when you are asked to read and think of your own ideas. These questions are called *evaluating* and *extending meaning* questions.

---

### This is the What Lights Up Strategy

1. **READ: Read** the question.

2. **FIND: Find** the facts you need in the story.

3. **DECIDE: Decide** which strategy to use.
   **Write: Write** the facts in the book.
   **Think: Think** about your own ideas.
   **Light Up:** Think about what you have written. The answer will **light up** in your mind.

4. **ANSWER:** Choose the best **answer.**

# Reading Comprehension

## Specific Objectives

**Objective 1: Determining word meanings**
*Prefixes and suffixes, context clues, technical words, and words with multiple meanings*

**Objective 2: Identifying supporting ideas**
*Recalling facts and details, sequential order, following directions, and describing settings*

**Objective 3: Summarizing main ideas**
*Stated and implied main ideas, and identifying summaries*

**Objective 4: Perceiving relationships and recognizing outcomes**
*Cause-and-effect and making predictions*

**Objective 5: Making inferences and generalizations**
*Interpreting graphs and diagrams, inferring information, drawing conclusions, making judgments, and evaluating plot*

**Objective 6: Recognizing points of view, facts, and opinions**
*Author's purpose, persuasive language, and discerning facts and points of view*

# Specific Objectives

## Objective 1: Determining Word Meanings

Prefixes and suffixes are parts of some words. A *prefix* appears at the beginning of a word. A *suffix* appears at the end of a word. Both prefixes and suffixes affect the meaning of the word. You can use them to help figure out the meaning of a word.

Phil went to the weight room almost every day after school. The trainer had told him that frequent workouts would strengthen his muscles.

**1    In this paragraph, the word strengthen means —**

    **A**    make weak.

    **B**    make strong.

    **C**    tire out.

    **D**    energize.

*Hint: The suffix "-en" means cause to be.*

There are two types of secret codes. In one kind of code, symbols take the place of letters. These symbols can be numbers, words, or even letters. A code book is used to read the message. The other kind of code changes the arrangement of the letters in a word. The letters have to be unscrambled to read the message.

**2    In this paragraph, the word arrangement means —**

    **F**    face.

    **G**    size.

    **H**    shape.

    **J**    order.

*Hint: The suffix "-ment" means the result of.*

Maya Lin drew a design for a monument for a contest. Her design won and was built. Thousands of names were carved on two walls of shiny black stone. The names were Americans who had died in the Vietnam War. At first, people thought that the stone was ugly. They disliked it. But then they began to change their minds. They found that they could walk up to the walls. They could touch the names of loved ones.

**3    What is the meaning of the word disliked?**

_____

_____

_____

_____

_____

_____

*Hint: "Dis-" is a prefix. It means the opposite of.*

None of the soldiers was prepared for the predawn drill. It seemed as though they had just fallen asleep. The sergeant disagreed and wanted them up, dressed, and ready to obey orders.

**4    In this paragraph, the word predawn means —**

    **A**    before daybreak.

    **B**    early.

    **C**    difficult.

    **D**    old.

*Hint: "Pre-" is a prefix. It means before.*

▶ **GO ON**

**Answers**

**1** Ⓐ Ⓑ Ⓒ Ⓓ     **2** Ⓕ Ⓖ Ⓗ Ⓙ     **4** Ⓐ Ⓑ Ⓒ Ⓓ

# Objective 1: Determining Word Meanings

Sometimes you can figure out the meaning of a new or difficult word by using the words around it as clues.

Sand that sits on top of clay in streams is called quicksand. The quicksand is <u>saturated</u> with water because the water cannot drain through the clay.

**1   In this paragraph, the word <u>saturated</u> means —**

    **A**   colored.

    **B**   reached.

    **C**   dried.

    **D**   soaked.

*Hint: You get a clue about what <u>saturated</u> means from the words around it.*

On the tip of each finger is a pattern of ridges. This pattern is called a *fingerprint*. Each finger has a <u>distinct</u> fingerprint. No two people in the world have the same fingerprints. A person's fingerprints always remain the same.

**2   In this paragraph, the word <u>distinct</u> means —**

    **F**   one-of-a-kind.

    **G**   silver.

    **H**   smooth.

    **J**   funny.

*Hint: You get a clue about what <u>distinct</u> means from the description of fingerprints.*

The rose has been a sign of <u>secrecy</u>. Hundreds of years ago, people wore roses behind their ears. It meant that the people wearing the roses had heard something, but would not tell what they had heard.

**3   In this paragraph, the word <u>secrecy</u> means —**

    **A**   riddles.

    **B**   silence.

    **C**   talking.

    **D**   sharing.

*Hint: You get a clue about what <u>secrecy</u> means by reading the last sentence in the paragraph.*

A <u>cavern</u> is a hole in the surface of the earth made by the forces of nature. People like to explore and hide things in these dark rooms and tunnels under the earth.

**4   What is another word for <u>cavern</u>?**

_____

_____

_____

_____

_____

_____

*Hint: You get a clue about what <u>cavern</u> means by reading the entire paragraph.*

▶GO ON

**Answers**
  **1** Ⓐ Ⓑ Ⓒ Ⓓ    **2** Ⓕ Ⓖ Ⓗ Ⓙ    **3** Ⓐ Ⓑ Ⓒ Ⓓ

# Objective 1: Determining Word Meanings

**Specialized or technical words are words used in subjects such as science and social studies. You can use all the other information in the text to help figure out the meaning of these words.**

Food on the frontier was simple. People ate many things made from flour. Flour was <u>nourishing</u> and did not spoil. Foods made from flour gave people energy to work hard.

**1    In this paragraph, the word <u>nourishing</u> means —**

    **A**    white.

    **B**    healthful.

    **C**    difficult.

    **D**    expensive.

*Hint:* <u>Nourishing</u> *is a technical word. You get a clue about what it means by reading the last sentence in the paragraph.*

How do pilots avoid <u>collisions</u> with other planes in the air? The sky is mapped into highways just like the land is. Signals are sent up from control towers to mark these "skyways." It's a pilot's job to listen to the signals.

**2    In this paragraph, the word <u>collisions</u> means —**

    **F**    birds.

    **G**    crashes.

    **H**    insects.

    **J**    tires.

*Hint:* <u>Collisions</u> *is a technical word. You get a clue about what it means from the entire paragraph.*

A Venus' flytrap is a plant that <u>consumes</u> bugs. When there are no bugs, this plant will gladly accept bits of cheese!

**3    In this paragraph, what does the word <u>consumes</u> mean?**

_____

_____

_____

_____

_____

_____

*Hint:* <u>Consumes</u> *is a technical word. You get a clue about what it means from the sentence after the word.*

**Answers**
**1** Ⓐ Ⓑ Ⓒ Ⓓ     **2** Ⓕ Ⓖ Ⓗ Ⓙ

The sound of a person's voice is <u>determined</u> by the length of his or her vocal cords. Most men have deeper voices than women. That's because men's vocal cords are longer. A tall person often has a deeper voice than a short person.

**4** **In this paragraph, the word <u>determined</u> means —**

    **A** decided.

    **B** hidden.

    **C** known.

    **D** heard.

*Hint:* <u>Determined</u> *is a technical term. You get a clue about what it means by reading the entire paragraph.*

Surgeons wore white uniforms until 1914. A doctor thought that the white uniform showed too much blood from <u>surgeries</u>. He wore green instead. Red did not show as much on the green.

**5** **In this paragraph, the word <u>surgeries</u> means —**

    **F** operations.

    **G** janitors.

    **H** movies.

    **J** straps.

*Hint:* <u>Surgeries</u> *is a technical word. You get a clue about what it means from the second sentence.*

We all have muscles <u>attached</u> to our outer ears. Some people work hard at moving these muscles. These are the people who can wiggle their ears! Can you do it?

**6** **What does the word <u>attached</u> mean in this paragraph?**

_____

_____

_____

_____

_____

_____

*Hint:* <u>Attached</u> *is a technical word. You get a clue about what it means by reading the entire paragraph.*

**STOP**

**Answers**
**4** Ⓐ Ⓑ Ⓒ Ⓓ    **5** Ⓕ Ⓖ Ⓗ Ⓙ

# Objective 2: Identifying Supporting Ideas

**Facts or details are important. By noticing and remembering them, you will know what the passage is about.**

Starfish of different sizes and colors live in the oceans. Starfish are often yellow, orange, or brown. But they can be bright colors, too. From point to point, a starfish can be as small as a paper clip or as long as a yardstick. Most starfish are shaped like stars, with five arms extending from their bodies. But some starfish, called sunstars, have a dozen arms. Other types have 25 arms.

1   **From point to point, a starfish can be the size of a —**

A   grain of rice.

B   car.

C   yardstick.

D   door.

*Hint: Look at the sentence that starts "From point to point."*

Tide pools are nature's aquariums. Ocean water flows inland with the tide. The water carries with it many living creatures. The water collects in hollows in rocks and in small holes in the earth. Tide pools are created when the tide goes out. The creatures stay behind in the pools.

2   **What causes ocean water to flow inland?**

_____

_____

_____

_____

_____

_____

*Hint: Look for the sentence that talks about the ocean water's flow.*

The last two steps in making toys are packaging and advertising them. Toy makers know that children like colorful objects. So they design bright packages for the toys. Writers think of catchy names for the toys. They hope children remember the names when they shop. With these steps completed, the toys are sent to toy stores. There, children decide whether or not a toy becomes a big seller.

3   **Toy makers know that colorful packages —**

F   are liked by children.

G   are assembled easily.

H   are cheap.

J   last a long time.

*Hint: Find the sentence about colorful packages.*

Our sun is one hundred times larger than Earth. But it is only a medium-sized star. The brightest, hottest stars are twenty times larger than the sun. They are called blue giants. Red dwarfs are stars that are smaller than our sun. These stars are the most common in the sky.

4   **Compared to Earth, the sun is —**

A   smaller.

B   the same size.

C   ten times larger.

D   one hundred times larger.

*Hint: Look for the sentence that talks about the sun's size.*

GO ON

**Answers**
1 Ⓐ Ⓑ Ⓒ Ⓓ    3 Ⓕ Ⓖ Ⓗ Ⓙ    4 Ⓐ Ⓑ Ⓒ Ⓓ

# Objective 2: Identifying Supporting Ideas

**Sometimes it is helpful to arrange events in the order they happened. This may help you to understand a passage better.**

In southern India, many people make a living by cutting and hauling wood. They could not do this without the help of trained elephants. Elephants are very smart. They can follow at least fifty different commands called out by the mahouts. A *mahout* is a person who works with elephants.

The mahouts first cut down the tall, heavy trees that grow on the mountains. They take bark from the logs. Next they drill a hole through a tree trunk and put a long, heavy chain through the hole. Then the mahouts tie a short rope to the chain.

Now the elephant takes over. A mahout sits on top of the elephant with his feet behind the elephant's ears. "Lift!" the mahout shouts. The big beast picks up the rope in its trunk and begins to drag the log. The heavy log may weigh as much as three and a half tons. This is about half the elephant's weight.

The elephant drags the log up a steep slope. All the time the mahout commands, "Lift the log over the rock! Walk straight!" The elephant often obeys, but it also thinks on its own. When the animal knows the ground is too slick, it changes direction. When the log gets stuck on a rock, the elephant drops the log, rolls it over, and picks it up again. The elephant does all this without being told.

At the top of the hill, the mahout shouts, "Drop the rope!" The elephant slowly lowers the log onto a huge pile of logs. Another mahout loosens the rope and chain. The animal then carries the mahout down the steep hill again.

The elephant may make this trip as many as thirty times each day. It is as strong as a small truck. But the elephant has what a truck does not have—brain power, common sense, and the ability to follow commands.

**1** **When does the elephant drag the log?**

**A** before the mahout shouts directions

**B** while the mahout cuts down the tree

**C** after the elephant picks up the rope

**D** before the mahout puts the chain through

*Hint: Sometimes it helps to write down the steps in order.*

**2** **When does the elephant take over?**

_____

_____

_____

_____

_____

*Hint: Find the paragraph that starts with this.*

**3** **Which of these happen first when cutting and hauling wood?**

**F** Mahouts attach chains to logs.

**G** Mahouts drill holes.

**H** Mahouts chop down trees.

**J** Mahouts take the bark from the logs.

*Hint: Look at the beginning of the passage.*

>GO ON

**Answers**
**1** Ⓐ Ⓑ Ⓒ Ⓓ     **3** Ⓕ Ⓖ Ⓗ Ⓙ

# Objective 2: Identifying Supporting Ideas

**Written directions tell you how to do something. Every step is important.**

When the wheel fell off their power mower, the Browns had to decide whether it was worth repairing or not. Mr. Brown examined all the wheels carefully. He decided that it was just a matter of time before another wheel fell off. He asked his son, Dave, to drain the oil from the motor. After that, Dave poured the gasoline remaining in the mower back into a gas can. Mrs. Brown shouted at them from the kitchen window, giving them directions. "I don't want the sanitation men to have any problems when they throw that mower into their truck!" she called to them. Dave pulled the old mower to the curb, thinking about the new one he'd be using in the future.

1 **Dave poured the gas from the mower into a gas can before —**

   **A** he brought it to the curb.

   **B** he drained the oil from the mower.

   **C** his father examined all the wheels.

   **D** the wheel fell off the mower.

*Hint: Find the sentence where Dave pours the gas into the can.*

2 **When did Mr. Brown decide the mower wasn't worth fixing?**

_____

_____

_____

_____

_____

_____

_____

*Hint: Find the sentence that tells about Mr. Brown's decision.*

**Answers**
1 (A) (B) (C) (D)

# Objective 2: Identifying Supporting Ideas

**The setting of a story lets you know when and where the story is taking place.**

Helen Klaben was the only passenger on the small plane that was flying from Alaska to Washington. She stared out the window at the swirling white snowstorm. It was February 4, 1963. Ralph Flores, the pilot of the plane, wasn't sure whether or not they were still on course. He dropped to a lower altitude to see better. He glanced down to change gas tanks. A moment later the plane crashed into some trees.

**1    When did the story take place?**

    **A**  in the fall

    **B**  in the winter

    **C**  in the summer

    **D**  in the spring

*Hint: Read the third sentence.*

**2    Where did the story take place?**

    **F**  in Alaska

    **G**  in Washington, D.C.

    **H**  in the state of Washington

    **J**  between Alaska and Washington

*Hint: Read the first sentence.*

In 1892, Chicago city leaders planned a fair. They wanted it to be the greatest fair ever. It would show the newest ideas in science, business, and art. They also wanted to build something grand at the fair. The Eiffel Tower had been built three years before in France. The Chicago leaders wanted something even grander. So they asked people to send in designs.

G.W. Ferris was a young engineer. He heard about the fair. He designed a wheel made of steel. The wheel was 250 feet across. Large cars hung from the end of each spoke. Each car could carry sixty people in a giant circle through the air.

On May 1, 1893, the fair opened. People came from around the world to see the latest inventions. They felt the heat of new electric stoves. They stood in the cool breeze of small fans. They saw a machine that washed dishes.

**3    Where did the fair open?**

    **A**  Paris, France

    **B**  Chicago, Illinois

    **C**  Elgin, Illinois

    **D**  Frankfurt, Germany

*Hint: Read the first paragraph.*

**4    When did the fair open?**

_____

_____

_____

*Hint: Read the first sentence of the third paragraph.*

**STOP**

Answers
1 (A) (B) (C) (D)    2 (F) (G) (H) (J)    3 (A) (B) (C) (D)

14

# Objective 3: Summarizing Main Ideas

**The main idea is the meaning of a piece of writing. Many times it is written in the passage.**

Most teenagers think their bodies have problems. Most girls think they are too fat. Eight out of ten girls go on diets before they are eighteen. Most teenage boys think they are too thin. They try to build up more muscles. Even if teenagers don't exactly think they are ugly, they would still like to make improvements. It takes teenagers a while to learn that their bodies are really all right the way they are.

**1    What is the main idea of this selection?**

   **A**  Girls can lose weight.

   **B**  Teenagers don't like the way they look.

   **C**  You can improve your looks.

   **D**  Teenage boys are skinny.

*Hint: What does the whole selection talk about?*

Fingerprints were not used as records until about 100 years ago. The English government began to keep the prints of its workers and prisoners. Sir Francis Galton made the first large collection of fingerprints. Because of Galton's work, police began to use fingerprints to track down criminals.

**2    What is the main idea of this selection?**

   **F**  Fingerprinting was started by the police.

   **G**  Scotland Yard began about 100 years ago.

   **H**  Police began to use fingerprints to track down criminals thanks to Sir Francis Galton's work.

   **J**  Records of fingerprints have been around for hundreds of years.

*Hint: What does the whole selection talk about?*

Scientists have been studying how people talk to each other. In one study, the scientists asked people about their feelings. Do people talk more about sad and angry feelings? Or do they talk more about happy and proud feelings? Scientists found out that people talk about unhappy feelings twice as much as happy ones.

**3    The main idea of this passage is to explain —**

   **A**  how to get over sad and angry feelings.

   **B**  what scientists have learned about feelings.

   **C**  which feelings people talk about most often.

   **D**  how often people brag about feeling unhappy.

*Hint: What is the point of the story?*

If gum ever sticks on your clothes, don't try to wash them. Otherwise, the gum may never come off. Put an ice cube on the gum. That will harden it, so you can try to scrape it off with a table knife. Try nail polish remover. It can sometimes melt gum. If the gum is from a bubble that burst, try chewing more gum and using it to lift off the stuck pieces.

**4    What is the main idea of this passage?**

_____

_____

_____

_____

_____

_____

_____

*Hint: What does the whole paragraph talk about?*

▶GO ON▶

**Answers**

**1** Ⓐ Ⓑ Ⓒ Ⓓ    **2** Ⓕ Ⓖ Ⓗ Ⓙ    **3** Ⓐ Ⓑ Ⓒ Ⓓ

15

# Objective 3: Summarizing Main Ideas

**Many times the main idea is not given in the text. Sometimes you need to figure it out by putting the facts together.**

Look under your kitchen sink. You will see some drain pipes. One pipe is U-shaped. It is called a trap. Harmful gases develop in a sewer line. The curved part of the trap holds a small amount of water. The water closes off the pipe. Then gases can't enter your house and harm you.

**1    The main idea of the paragraph is that a trap —**

    **A**   is a straight pipe.

    **B**   lets harmful gases enter your home.

    **C**   is not part of the drain pipe.

    **D**   has a very useful purpose.

*Hint: If you put all the facts together, what do they say about the trap?*

Electricity moves through wires in houses and buildings. This electrical flow is called a *current*. When a switch is on, the electric current can flow to machines and light fixtures. Then, the electric machines and lights can work. When a switch is off, the electric current doesn't flow. Then, electric machines can't work.

**2    What is the main idea in this selection?**

    **F**   If a switch is off, an electric machine will not work.

    **G**   Switches control electric current.

    **H**   If a switch is off, an electric machine will work.

    **J**   Switches are dangerous.

*Hint: Read the entire paragraph.*

Jackie Cochran was a natural pilot. She often flew in closed-circuit races. Closed circuit means that the course is round. The plane has to be flown with great skill. In 1940, Cochran broke the 2,000 kilometer closed-circuit world speed record. Then in 1947, she set a new 100 kilometer closed-circuit speed record. In 1953, she became the first woman to fly faster than the speed of sound.

**3    What is the main idea of this passage?**

_____

_____

_____

_____

_____

_____

_____

*Hint: What does the entire passage talk about?*

# Objective 3: Summarizing Main Ideas

**A good summary contains the main idea of a passage. It is brief, yet it covers the most important points.**

Our brain makes our lungs breathe and tells our muscles how to move. We use it to learn and remember. But even though it does so much, our brain weighs only about three pounds. Scientists say we use only a small part of it. They want to know what we do with the rest.

**1   What is this passage mostly about?**

   **A**  We use only a small part of our brain to do many things.

   **B**  The brain does not weigh very much.

   **C**  People can be smart.

   **D**  We use our brain to breathe.

*Hint: Which choice sums up the passage?*

If you sneeze, you'll almost always hear someone say "Bless you." Some historians think that people started saying "Bless you" over 1,000 years ago in Europe. At that time, the plague was spreading everywhere. One of the first signs of this terrible disease was sneezing. People thought the blessing might keep them from getting sick.

**2   What is this selection mostly about?**

_____

_____

_____

_____

_____

_____

_____

_____

*Hint: Which sentence tells you about the whole passage?*

**Answers**
1  Ⓐ Ⓑ Ⓒ Ⓓ

Only about one out of every ten people is left-handed. In ancient times people thought lefties were witches. Not so long ago, people thought they might be crooks. Now scientists have proven that those ideas are not true. In fact, left-handers may be more creative than right-handers.

**3  What is this selection mostly about?**

F   People think a lot about right-handed people.

G   Left-handed people have been thought about differently over the years.

H   Most witches and crooks are left-handed.

J   Left-handed people are the most creative kind.

*Hint: Which sentence tells you about the whole passage?*

Maybe you have seen flamingos in a zoo. These brightly colored birds with long necks look too pink to be real. Wild flamingos get their bright-pink feathers from the plants and fish they eat. However, in zoos they don't eat the same things that they eat in the wild. They could turn white. To keep this from happening, the zookeepers give these birds a special pill.

**4  What is this story mostly about?**

_____

_____

_____

_____

_____

_____

_____

_____

*Hint: What does the whole passage talk about?*

STOP

**Answers**
3  Ⓕ Ⓖ Ⓗ Ⓙ

# Objective 4: Perceiving Relationships and Recognizing Outcomes

**Knowing what made something happen or why a character did something will help you to understand what you read.**

Sea birds like to flock at an airport in Canada, and often they crash into airplanes. They break glass, damage engines, and cause accidents. Trained falcons can help to keep the sea birds out of the way. The air traffic controller tells the falcon trainer where the flocks of sea birds are. Then the trainer lets a falcon go. The fierce little bird flies very fast. It scares the sea birds away.

**1    When do the sea birds get scared away?**

    **A**  at the airport in Canada

    **B**  by the airplanes

    **C**  when a falcon is let go

    **D**  when the falcon trainer meets the air traffic controller

*Hint: What happens right before the birds get scared away?*

The Aztecs of Mexico played a ball game hundreds of years ago. When a player made a score, people watching had to give the player some of their clothes. The teams tried very hard to win. If a team lost, the team captains had to give up their heads.

**2    What made the team captains give up their heads?**

    **F**  They wanted more clothes.

    **G**  They wanted to win.

    **H**  They were showing off for the people watching.

    **J**  Their team lost.

*Hint: Something happened right before the team captains had to give up their heads. What was it?*

When their enemies chase them, ostriches lie down on the sand. The giant birds stretch their necks out flat on the ground. When they do that, the loose feathers on their bodies look like bushes. But ostriches don't need to hide often. Their strong legs are good for both running and fighting.

**3    What makes ostriches lie down on the sand?**

_____

_____

_____

_____

_____

_____

_____

_____

*Hint: What happens right before they lie down?*

Lots of movies use special effects. Many of these effects are the work of makeup artists. They sometimes use special materials, such as plastic. But often, they use simple things, such as food. When a script calls for fake blood, the artist mixes red food coloring, corn syrup, and peanut butter. This mixture looks real.

**4    What makes the mixture look real?**

    **A**  The artist uses plastic.

    **B**  The artist uses only food.

    **C**  The artist uses red food coloring, corn syrup, and peanut butter.

    **D**  The artist uses special materials.

*Hint: Certain things were used to make the mixture look real. What were they?*

**Answers**

1 Ⓐ Ⓑ Ⓒ Ⓓ    2 Ⓕ Ⓖ Ⓗ Ⓙ    4 Ⓐ Ⓑ Ⓒ Ⓓ

Sneakers were invented more than 100 years ago. They were called "croquet sandals." They cost five times as much as other shoes, so only rich people wore them. Then a company began to make tennis oxfords. Most people could afford these. They were very popular. Soon special sneakers were made for other sports, such as running. Now we have all sorts of sneakers.

**5** **What made tennis oxfords popular?**

    **F** They were made for running.

    **G** Most people could afford them.

    **H** They cost five times as much as other shoes.

    **J** They were called croquet sandals.

*Hint: Something is stated in the selection right before it says they were very popular. What is it?*

Ballet dancers often spin around and around, but they don't become dizzy. A dancer's body turns smoothly. But the dancer holds his or her head still and then jerks it around quickly. This way the head is still most of the time, and the dancer does not become dizzy.

**6** **Why don't ballet dancers become dizzy?**

    **A** They turn their heads smoothly.

    **B** Their heads are still most of the time.

    **C** Their bodies turn smoothly.

    **D** They don't spin around and around much.

*Hint: Read the last sentence.*

The Dead Sea is not really a sea. It is a large lake. The Dead Sea lies between Israel and Jordan. It is the lowest place on Earth. The surface is 1,292 feet below sea level. The water is very salty. It's saltier than ocean water. It is called the Dead Sea because fish can't live in the salty water.

**7** **Why is this lake called the Dead Sea?**

_____

_____

_____

_____

_____

_____

_____

*Hint: The answer is stated in the passage.*

GO ON

**Answers**
**5** Ⓕ Ⓖ Ⓗ Ⓙ    **6** Ⓐ Ⓑ Ⓒ Ⓓ

# Objective 4: Perceiving Relationships and Recognizing Outcomes

**Many times you can predict, or tell in advance, what is probably going to happen next. You must think about what would make sense if the story were to go on.**

Wanda did not get many new clothes. Usually they were handed down from her big sister or older cousins. On her birthday, her mother gave her a beautiful dress handmade from pieces of things she had outgrown. Wanda was very proud of it and wore it to school the next day. But there, the other kids laughed at her and called her new dress a bunch of rags.

**1  What is likely to happen next?**

**A** Wanda will laugh.

**B** Wanda will never wear the dress to school again.

**C** Wanda will have her mother make dresses for the other girls.

**D** Wanda will give the dress to someone else.

*Hint: Think about what you would most likely do if you were Wanda.*

Mr. Henry's class had been studying birds. The class decided to go bird watching. They walked along a trail in the woods. Suddenly Mr. Henry told them to stop a few minutes. When they were quiet, they could hear a loud pecking sound.

**2  What is Mr. Henry most likely to do?**

**F** point a woodpecker out to the class

**G** ask the class to act like woodpeckers

**H** leave the woods immediately with the class

**J** start to make loud noises

*Hint: Think about what the noise is.*

It was a hot summer day. Andres and Nicole asked their mom if they could play in the sprinkler. She agreed. As they went outside, she reminded them to turn off the water when they were finished. They ran out to the backyard, turned on the sprinkler, and ran in and out of the sprinkler for about an hour. Then they decided to ride bikes. When they came home, their mother stood at the door with her arms crossed in front of her.

**3  What will their mother do next and why?**

_____

_____

_____

_____

_____

_____

_____

*Hint: Once you figure out why their mother is standing at the door, you will know the answer.*

>GO ON>

**Answers**
1 (A) (B) (C) (D)    2 (F) (G) (H) (J)

21

Julio had helped his grandfather cut hay all day. It had been another long, hot day, and he was glad to drive the tractor into the cool barn. He walked to the porch, where his grandfather handed him a pitcher of lemonade and a glass.

**4    What will Julio probably do next?**

   **A**  take the pitcher and the glass into the house

   **B**  pour the lemonade into the glass

   **C**  give the pitcher and glass back to his grandfather

   **D**  put the pitcher and glass down and go back to the barn

*Hint: Think about what you would do.*

Monique loved bananas. She loved banana splits, pudding, and ice cream. But her favorite way to eat a banana was simply to peel it and eat it. One day, she had just enjoyed her favorite food while sitting on the front steps of her house. She left the peel on the steps. An hour later, her mother came home and climbed the steps to the house. Monique heard a scream.

**5    What probably happened?**

   **F**  Her mother slipped on the peel.

   **G**  Her mother realized they needed more bananas.

   **H**  Her mother wanted Monique to know she came home.

   **J**  Her mother was greeted by a stranger at the front door.

*Hint: Which of the choices makes the most sense?*

Gabriela helped her father repaint her room. First, they moved all the furniture into the middle of the room and covered it with plastic sheets. Then, they brought in ladders. They spread out old newspapers on the floor. Then, they opened a can of paint and stirred it.

**6    What will Gabriela and her father probably do next?**

_____

_____

_____

_____

_____

_____

_____

*Hint: You need to read the entire paragraph and especially the last sentence.*

STOP

**Answers**
   **4**  Ⓐ Ⓑ Ⓒ Ⓓ       **5**  Ⓕ Ⓖ Ⓗ Ⓙ

22

# Objective 5: Making Inferences and Generalizations

Sometimes a passage will have a graph or diagram with it. These are there to help you understand the passage.

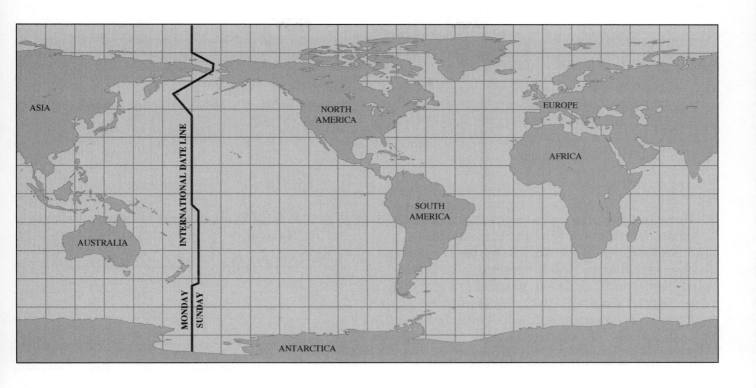

The international date line is a line on a map. It is the ending line for measuring time zones. On one side of the international date line, it is one day. On the other side of the international date line, it is a day later or earlier. The international date line does not always follow a straight line. If it followed a straight line, it would cross land. This would cause problems for the people living in these areas.

1   According to the map, if the international date line were straight, which continent would it go through?

   A   Asia

   B   Africa

   C   Europe

   D   North America

*Hint: Look for each choice on the map and mark it.*

2   What day will it be in North America if it is Tuesday in Asia?

_____

_____

_____

_____

_____

_____

_____

*Hint: Look at the map to see where each continent is.*

GO ON

**Answers**
1 Ⓐ Ⓑ Ⓒ Ⓓ

**KEY EVENTS IN MEXICO'S HISTORY**

The Olmecs, Mexico's first great civilization, flourished.

The Aztecs dominated Mexico.

Mexico became independent from Spain.

The Mexican Revolution started.

Mexico signed the North American Free Trade Agreement with Canada and the United States.

| 1200–400 B.C. | A.D. 300–900 | 1428–1521 | 1519 | 1821 | 1846–48 | 1910 | 1938 | 1994 |

The Mayas' "Classical Period," when the great temples and pyramids were built.

The first Spaniards arrived, beginning the conquest.

Mexico lost half its territory in a war with the United States.

Mexico expelled foreign oil companies and nationalized the industry.

Some of the world's greatest civilizations lived in Mexico. The Olmecs were the earliest culture, and they lasted until 400 B.C. The Mayas were next, and built great temples and pyramids. The Aztecs ruled Mexico until 1521, two years after the arrival of the Spanish invaders. The Aztecs built cities with highly organized societies. Mexico remained under Spanish rule for 300 years.

**3** Look at the time line. What year did Mexico gain its independence?

**F** 400 B.C.

**G** 1519

**H** 1521

**J** 1821

*Hint: Check each choice on the time line.*

**4** Why is Spanish the national language of Mexico?

_____

_____

_____

_____

_____

_____

_____

_____

*Hint: Use the time line to help you.*

▶ GO ON

**Answers**
**3** Ⓕ Ⓖ Ⓗ Ⓙ

# Objective 5: Making Inferences and Generalizations

A logical conclusion is an ending that makes sense. Many times it can be proved by the information given in the paragraph.

Lisa Meitner was born in Austria in 1878. She grew up to be a famous scientist. In college, she studied atoms. After college, she began to work with the great scientist Max Planck. Later, she pioneered the splitting of the atom. But Meitner saw the war-like side of her research. She would not help make the atom bomb.

1  The passage suggests that Lisa Meitner —

   A  was against using her research for harmful purposes.

   B  did not know how to make a bomb.

   C  never knew much about atoms.

   D  was born in Australia.

   *Hint: Read the last two sentences.*

Where is the safest place to be during a thunderstorm? You might think your house would be the best place. However, you are safer in a car than in a house. If lightning strikes a car, it spreads over the metal and runs through the tires into the ground. Of course, you should not touch metal parts of the car if lightning strikes it.

2  From this passage, you can tell that lightning —

   F  does not strike cars.

   G  probably won't harm the inside of a car.

   H  makes a car run better.

   J  does not strike houses.

   *Hint: Pick the choice that can be proved by what's in the passage.*

Reggie Jackson was one of the best baseball players of all time. He always played well in the World Series. In the early 1970s, he played for the Oakland A's. He led the team to victory in three World Series. Then he was traded to the New York Yankees. He led the Yankees into three World Series, too. The Yankees won two of those World Series. In one game, Jackson hit three home runs. Because of this, he became known as Mr. October.

3  When is the World Series held? Which clue did you use?

   _____

   _____

   _____

   _____

   _____

   _____

   *Hint: A sentence in the passage will help you answer the question.*

>GO ON>

Answers
1  Ⓐ Ⓑ Ⓒ Ⓓ    2  Ⓕ Ⓖ Ⓗ Ⓙ

25

Do you know about the Seven Wonders of the Ancient World? These structures were built long, long ago. One was the Lighthouse of Pharos in Egypt. It stood over 400 feet tall. Another was the Colossus of Rhodes on an island near Turkey. This bronze statue was almost 200 feet tall. All but one of these wonders have disappeared. You can still see the Great Pyramids in Egypt.

**4** **The story suggests that —**

   **A**  the Colossus was in Egypt.

   **B**  six of the ancient wonders no longer exist.

   **C**  the Great Pyramids have disappeared.

   **D**  the Colossus was taller than the Lighthouse.

*Hint: Pick the choice that can be proved true.*

At the age of three, Louis Braille lost his sight. But he did not let this loss stand in his way. As a teenager, he became an accomplished musician. At age 19, Braille began teaching the blind in Paris. One year later, in 1829, he developed a system of printing. The Braille system uses 63 sets of 6 raised dots. This system, often called Braille, is still used today.

**5** **The Braille system —**

   **F**  is helpful to the deaf.

   **G**  is used by everyone today.

   **H**  can be read by touch.

   **J**  cannot be used by the blind.

*Hint: Which choice makes the most sense?*

Alfred Wegener looked at a world map. He noticed a strange thing. All the continents looked like jigsaw pieces. All the pieces seemed to fit together. Wegener thought about this idea for a long time. In 1912, he offered a new theory. He claimed that all the continents were once a large land mass. Then, over time, the continents moved apart. Wegener called his theory "continental drift." But other scientists did not accept his ideas until forty years later.

**6** **Why did Wegener offer his new theory?**

_____

_____

_____

_____

_____

_____

*Hint: Read sentences 7 and 8.*

>GO ON>

# Objective 5: Making Inferences and Generalizations

The way a person acts tells you about the character's mood. Other clues may be what is said or how the character responds to what happens in the passage.

In the 1930s, African-American nurses could not care for white soldiers. Mabel Staupers wanted to change this problem. She asked for help from the Red Cross and many nursing groups. Still, Staupers did not succeed. But she kept struggling. Then World War II broke out. As the war got worse, more nurses were needed. By 1945, the armed forces nursing corps were fully integrated. Mabel Staupers had achieved her goal at last.

**1    When Mabel Staupers could not care for white soldiers, she probably felt —**

A    angry.

B    happy.

C    amused.

D    relieved.

*Hint: Think about what she did later.*

Tamara ran her finger down the first column on the page. "No, no, no," she repeated over and over. Suddenly her finger stopped on one of the little boxes. "Two rooms with a large kitchen," she read. Then she circled the box of print with her pen and called to her sister, "I think I've finally found something!"

**2    You know from this selection that Tamara is —**

F    excited.

G    depressed.

H    interested in becoming a newspaper reporter.

J    mad at her sister.

*Hint: Read the words Tamara uses to express herself.*

Mel studied his son. He wondered what he could say to convince the boy not to take the job. Mel knew the job seemed wonderful to a boy in high school. How could he explain to his son that it was more important to wait until he finished school?

**3    How does Mel feel about his son's job offer?**

_____

_____

_____

_____

_____

_____

_____

*Hint: Figure out what Mel wants his son to do.*

**Answers**
1 Ⓐ Ⓑ Ⓒ Ⓓ     2 Ⓕ Ⓖ Ⓗ Ⓙ

In 1916, a great fire swept through northern Ontario. It left behind 1,000 square miles of burned forests and farmland. Six Canadian towns were burned, too. Bob Foster watched the fire as it neared. Seeing its fury, he lay face down in a potato patch as the fire roared around him. The smoke and heat were awful, but Bob survived the fire unharmed.

**4** **How did Bob feel after the fire was out?**

A grateful

B afraid

C furious

D great

*Hint: Think about how you might feel.*

Ken sat with his hands clenching the armrests. The woman in the aisle said, "Please fasten your seat belts." Ken fumbled with the belt. The woman then made sure all the seats were in an upright position. She finished just as the engines began to roar on either side of Ken. He checked to make sure that there was an air sickness bag in the pocket in front of him.

**5** **How does Ken feel about flying?**

_____

_____

_____

_____

_____

_____

_____

_____

*Hint: Think about why Ken did all the things he did.*

STOP

# Objective 6: Recognizing Points of View, Facts, and Opinions

It is important to know the difference between fact and opinion. A fact is real and true. An opinion is a feeling or belief. Words that describe are used to offer opinions.

Rubber comes from a rubber tree. White juice, called *latex*, drips out of holes in the tree. Today, latex is used to make many things, such as rubber gloves and paint. People in Mexico were the first to use latex. One thing they did with latex was make shoes. They dipped their feet in the latex and let it dry.

**1    Which of the following is an OPINION based on the passage?**

   **A**   Mexican people made rubber shoes.

   **B**   Rubber comes from a tree.

   **C**   The people in Mexico had good ideas.

   **D**   People dipped their feet in latex.

   *Hint: Which choice is a feeling or belief?*

Power lawn mowers make lawn care easy. Years ago, people had to push a mower by hand. The push mower had three long blades, which were attached to wheels on both sides. As the wheels turned, the blades spun and cut the grass. It took a long time to cut a lawn, especially when the grass was high. You had to be strong to push a mower like that. Today power lawn mowers come in all sizes. Some are so large that a person can ride on them.

**2    Which of these is an OPINION from the passage?**

   **F**   Power lawn mowers make lawn care easier.

   **G**   A push mower has three long blades.

   **H**   You can ride some power mowers.

   **J**   Mowers come in many sizes.

   *Hint: Which choice is a feeling?*

Pocahontas was the daughter of the Native American chief Powatan. She made friends with the English settlers who came to Virginia in the early 1600s. One day, their leader, John Smith, was captured by her tribe. Pocahontas risked her life to save him. She also brought the settlers food to keep them from starving. Later, she married John Smith. She helped keep peace between her tribe and the settlers.

**3    Which of these is a FACT from the passage?**

   **A**   Pocahontas was a fearful person.

   **B**   Pocahontas was of mixed heritage.

   **C**   Pocahontas only liked one of the English settlers.

   **D**   Pocahontas gave food to the settlers.

   *Hint: Facts are real and true.*

▶GO ON▶

Answers
   1  Ⓐ Ⓑ Ⓒ Ⓓ      2  Ⓕ Ⓖ Ⓗ Ⓙ      3  Ⓐ Ⓑ Ⓒ Ⓓ

Everyone knows what a tiger is. And everyone has heard of lions. But do you know what a liger is? A liger is a cross between a lion and a tiger. In 1948, the first liger was born in the United States. It was born at the Hagh Zoo in Salt Lake City, Utah.

**4** **Which of the following is an OPINION based on the passage?**

    **F** A liger is a cross between a tiger and a lion.

    **G** Many people do not like ligers.

    **H** Ligers did not exist before 1948.

    **J** Most ligers live in zoos.

*Hint: Which statement is a feeling?*

Essie's favorite tree had blown over in a wind storm. She had always loved the graceful weeping willow tree. Her dad suggested that she plant a new one. They went to a tree farm where they picked out a young tree. When they got home, they dug a wide, deep hole and placed the new tree gently into it. Then they watered it thoroughly while covering its roots with dirt.

**5** **Which of these is a FACT from the passage?**

    **A** Essie liked willow trees more than oaks.

    **B** Essie's tree was blown over in a storm.

    **C** Essie's dad was glad the tree had blown over.

    **D** It's very hard for two people to plant a tree.

*Hint: Which choice is real and true?*

**STOP**

Directions: Read each selection carefully. Then read each question. Darken the circle for the correct answer, or write the answer in the space provided.

| TRY THIS | More than one answer choice may seem correct. Choose the answer that goes <u>best</u> with the selection. |
|---|---|

Sample A

### Going to the Store

Ross and Drew went to the store to buy milk. Ross had a dollar in his pocket. He used the dollar to pay for the milk.

What did Ross have in his pocket?

A  a dime

B  milk

C  a dollar

D  a map

| THINK IT THROUGH | The correct answer is <u>C</u>. The second sentence in the story says that Ross had <u>a dollar</u> in his pocket. The story does not say that Ross had a dime, milk, or a map in his pocket. |
|---|---|

**STOP**

### The Butterfly

There are many kinds of butterflies. Some live only for a few weeks. Others live for several months or years. Some butterflies are yellow or green. They look like leaves. They can hide in the trees or in plants. Others have bright colors. All these butterflies help make our world more colorful.

1  From this story you know that —

A  all butterflies live for a long time.

B  there are only a few kinds of butterflies.

C  all butterflies hide in trees.

D  there are many different kinds of butterflies.

2  Why do butterflies hide?

_____

_____

_____

_____

_____

_____

**GO ON**

Answers
SA Ⓐ Ⓑ Ⓒ Ⓓ     1 Ⓐ Ⓑ Ⓒ Ⓓ

# The Man Behind the Bear

Have you ever heard of Morris Michtom? You may not have heard of him, but you almost certainly have heard about a toy he invented. Michtom and his family came to the United States from Russia. They lived in Brooklyn, New York, where Michtom owned a small candy, novelty, and stationery store.

Michtom greatly admired Theodore Roosevelt, who was the President of the United States at that time. In 1902, Michtom read a newspaper story about Roosevelt. The story told how, during a hunting trip, the President saved a small bear cub from being shot. A cartoon of the event accompanied the story. The cartoon and story gave Michtom an idea for a new toy.

Michtom wrote a letter to President Roosevelt. He asked the President's permission to make and sell a stuffed toy bear cub called the "Teddy Bear." The President wrote back to Michtom and gave his permission. Rose Michtom, Morris' wife, made the first bear for sale with movable arms and legs. It sold quickly, and she made more bears to replace it. Michtom soon formed a new company to produce more of the teddy bears.

Teddy bears became popular all over the United States. Today, many different kinds of stuffed bears are made and sold to both children and adults. Michtom's toy company is still in business today in Brooklyn, New York.

GO ON

**3** What is this selection mainly about?

    **F** Morris Michtom's life in Russia

    **G** how a toy company is operated

    **H** how the teddy bear was invented

    **J** President Roosevelt's hunting trip

**4** How did Michtom make a living in Brooklyn?

    **A** He owned a small store.

    **B** He wrote newspaper stories.

    **C** He worked for the President.

    **D** He owned a toy store.

**5** Where did Morris Michtom first get his idea?

_____

_____

_____

_____

_____

_____

_____

**6** The toy company started by Michtom—

    **F** is now owned by the government.

    **G** closed down when Roosevelt left office.

    **H** never was very successful.

    **J** is still in business today.

**7** Today, teddy bears are—

    **A** not very popular.

    **B** bought by many children and adults.

    **C** hard-to-find items.

    **D** sold only in Brooklyn.

**8** What did Michtom do first after he got his idea?

    **F** He formed a company.

    **G** He started selling teddy bears.

    **H** He read a newspaper story.

    **J** He wrote to President Roosevelt.

**9** Where would this selection most likely be found?

    **A** in a children's book

    **B** in a farmer's almanac

    **C** in a history book

    **D** in an autobiography

**10** What is another good title for this story?

    **F** "The Beginnings of the Teddy Bear"

    **G** "Save the Bears"

    **H** "All About President Theodore Roosevelt"

    **J** "From Russia to New York"

GO ON

**Answers**

**3** Ⓕ Ⓖ Ⓗ Ⓙ     **6** Ⓕ Ⓖ Ⓗ Ⓙ     **8** Ⓕ Ⓖ Ⓗ Ⓙ     **10** Ⓕ Ⓖ Ⓗ Ⓙ

**4** Ⓐ Ⓑ Ⓒ Ⓓ     **7** Ⓐ Ⓑ Ⓒ Ⓓ     **9** Ⓐ Ⓑ Ⓒ Ⓓ

# Making Papier-Mâché

Papier-mâché is easy to make and fun to use. If you use your imagination, you can create just about anything you want with papier-mâché. Here's how you make papier-mâché:

1. Gather newspaper, scissors, flour, water, a spoon, and a bowl.
2. Cut or tear the newspaper into strips.
3. Mix a cup of flour and half a cup of water in the bowl until the mixture is smooth.
4. Dip the newspaper into the flour and water mixture until it is completely wet.
5. Then form the wet newspaper into the shape you want. You can make animals, bowls, jewelry, masks, and many other things in this way.
6. Let the wet papier-mâché dry for several days. It will become very hard.
7. Paint the papier-mâché and decorate it with colored paper, feathers, or buttons if you like.

**11** Which of these is *not* necessary when making papier-mâché?

    **A** letting the papier-mâché objects dry for several days

    **B** dipping the newspaper strips into the mixture

    **C** using paint and colored paper to decorate the papier-mâché objects

    **D** forming the wet newspaper into a shape

**12** Which of the following would *not* be a good choice to make from papier-mâché?

    **F** masks

    **G** jewelry

    **H** bowls

    **J** clothing

**13** What is used to make papier-mâché?

    **A** flour, newspaper, and water

    **B** newspaper, salt, and soda

    **C** feathers, buttons, and colored paper

    **D** milk, butter, and eggs

**14** How long does it take for the papier-mâché to dry?

_____

_____

_____

_____

_____

_____

_____

_____

**GO ON**

# Brothers

Seth and his big brother Frank were walking along the beach. Frank was home from college for the summer. The boys had time on their hands. As they walked, Seth picked up an oyster shell.

"This reminds me of those great smoked oysters Dad made last fall," said Seth.

"You have always loved oysters," laughed Frank. "Let me tell you what I learned about oysters this year."

Frank picked up an oyster shell and turned it over in his hand. "Did you know that baby oysters do not have shells? They are little, round creatures, about the size of the head of a pin. They swim around by moving tiny hairs on their bodies. When an oyster is one day old, it starts to form a hard shell. In about a week, the shell is fully formed. That is when the oyster finds a rock to attach itself to. It stays there for the rest of its life.

"The oyster shell is really two shells. They are held together by a hinge, which is part of the oyster's body. When the lid of the shell is open, the oyster is in danger. You see, you are not the only one that likes to eat them. Many sea animals love oysters, too.

"The oyster has no eyes or ears. Tiny feelers tell the oyster when it is in danger. When this happens, the shell lid slams shut, keeping the oyster safe inside. Many hungry fish, seals, and otters have been turned away by a tightly shut oyster shell."

"You do know a lot about oysters," said Seth. "What else did you learn?"

"Well," said Frank, "oysters are members of a family called mollusks. Mollusks all have soft bodies without bones. Clams and snails are also members of this family. Other mollusks, such as octopuses and slugs, do not have shells."

"Frank, I hate to cut this walk short," said Seth. "But all your talk about oysters is making me hungry. Let's head home for lunch."

---

**15** About how long does it take for an oyster shell to fully form?

_____

_____

_____

_____

**16** Which of these events was happening as the story took place?

**F** Frank was arriving home from college.

**G** Seth was eating smoked oysters.

**H** Seth and Frank were walking.

**J** Seth and Frank were fishing.

**17** Which words in the story tell that Seth and Frank were in no hurry?

**A** …had time on their hands.

**B** Let me tell you what I learned…

**C** What else…

**D** Let's head home…

**18** Which statement about baby oysters is *not* true?

**F** They are small and round.

**G** They are surrounded by a soft shell.

**H** They swim by moving tiny hairs.

**J** They are about the size of the head of a pin.

**Answers**
**16** Ⓕ Ⓖ Ⓗ Ⓙ   **17** Ⓐ Ⓑ Ⓒ Ⓓ   **18** Ⓕ Ⓖ Ⓗ Ⓙ

# Volunteer Jobs

## Wanted: Good Readers!

Tuesday afternoons 3:30–4:00
See Ms. Chung in Room 114.

Are you a good reader? If so, join the Reading Talent Club, and volunteer to read books aloud for younger children. We will make cassette recordings of books to be used by kindergarteners and first graders. Make books come alive for beginning readers!

## Save the Planet

Wednesday mornings 7:15–7:45 or
Thursday afternoons 3:30–4:00
Choose one or both times.
See Mr. Titan in Room 211.

Help take care of our Earth by picking up litter on the school grounds and managing the school recycling center. If you are Earth-friendly, Earth Patrol is for you!

## Food Collection

The last Monday afternoon of each month 3:30–4:30
See Ms. Nethercutt in Room 118.

Help collect and sort food to be distributed to community members in need. Join the food drive to help drive out hunger in your community!

## Help Others!

Wednesday afternoons 3:30–5:00
See Ms. Rios in Room 109.

If you enjoy helping others, think about joining Community Outreach. We'll make get-well cards for children in hospitals and write letters to people in military service. We'll spend a good deal of time practicing a musical. At the end of the year, we'll travel to a local nursing home to perform the musical for residents.

GO ON

**19** Which group has meetings in the morning?

_____

_____

_____

_____

_____

_____

_____

**20** Which group is *not* mentioned in the notices?

**A** Safety Patrol

**B** Community Outreach

**C** Reading Talent

**D** Earth Patrol

**21** Which group has choices for meeting times?

**F** Community Outreach

**G** Food Collection

**H** Earth Patrol

**J** Reading Talent

**22** Which group will take a field trip?

**A** Reading Talent

**B** Earth Patrol

**C** Community Outreach

**D** Food Collection

**23** When does the Food Collection meet?

**F** every Monday afternoon

**G** Wednesday mornings

**H** Tuesday afternoons

**J** the last Monday afternoon of the month

**24** All of the Volunteer Jobs —

**A** meet once a week.

**B** provide help to students at school.

**C** practice a musical.

**D** have teacher sponsors.

**25** Who should you contact if you want to join Earth Patrol?

**F** Ms. Chung

**G** Mr. Titan

**H** Ms. Nethercutt

**J** Ms. Rios

**26** Which of the following is *not* true of "Wanted: Good Readers!"

**A** Members will record books on tape.

**B** See Ms. Chung to join.

**C** The tapes will be used by younger children.

**D** Members will learn how to read.

>GO ON>

**Answers**

| **20** Ⓐ Ⓑ Ⓒ Ⓓ | **22** Ⓐ Ⓑ Ⓒ Ⓓ | **24** Ⓐ Ⓑ Ⓒ Ⓓ | **26** Ⓐ Ⓑ Ⓒ Ⓓ |
| **21** Ⓕ Ⓖ Ⓗ Ⓙ | **23** Ⓕ Ⓖ Ⓗ Ⓙ | **25** Ⓕ Ⓖ Ⓗ Ⓙ | |

37

# Edgardo's Rescue

Edgardo pursued the giant yellow and black butterfly into the field. It was a Tiger Swallowtail, the kind he had been wanting for his collection. What luck to find it so easily! Edgardo was about to swing the butterfly net when his dog Tag started barking loudly at something in the brush. Edgardo looked in that direction, and the butterfly escaped into the sky.

"You worthless dog!" he exclaimed. "What is the matter with you?" Edgardo realized it was his own fault that he had lost the butterfly. He should not have looked away. Still, he wanted to blame somebody.

Suddenly, Edgardo saw what had made Tag bark. A tiny, spotted fawn, no more than a week old, lay nestled in a thicket. It seemed to be *abandoned*, and Edgardo wondered if Tag had chased the mother away. The baby looked very small, alone, and confused.

Then Edgardo remembered something he had read. Mother deer often leave their fawns hidden in the woods for short periods of time while they go off to feed. The doe would probably come back soon. Edgardo grabbed his dog by the collar and told him, "Time to go home, Tag." Tag whined. He wanted to remain right there. Edgardo did, too, in a way. He wanted to be sure the doe would return.

A week later, Edgardo returned to check on the fawn. This time he made sure that Tag stayed behind. First, he looked in the thicket, hoping that the fawn had survived the week. He saw an area of mashed-down brush at the spot where he had first seen the fawn. That revealed to him that the fawn was sleeping there every night, and Edgardo relaxed. The mother had been close by after all. He could stop being concerned and go back to working on his butterfly collection.

**27** **Why did Edgardo want to stay?**

**F** He wanted to make Tag happy.

**G** He wanted another chance to catch the butterfly.

**H** He wanted to make sure that the fawn's mother would return.

**J** He wanted to hide from his brother.

**28** **When did Edgardo return?**

**A** later that day

**B** in a month

**C** the next day

**D** a week later

**29** **What was Edgardo most concerned about?**

_____

_____

_____

_____

**30** **Why did Edgardo lose the Tiger Swallowtail?**

**F** He tripped over the fawn.

**G** Tag barked and scared the butterfly.

**H** There was a hole in his net.

**J** He looked away to see why Tag was barking.

**31** **In this selection, the word** *abandoned* **means—**

**A** hungry.          **C** thirsty.

**B** tired.            **D** left behind.

**32** **Which of these most likely happened after Edgardo went home?**

**F** The doe returned to its fawn.

**G** Someone took the fawn home.

**H** Tag found another deer.

**J** The doe and fawn followed Edgardo home.

STOP

**Answers**
**27** Ⓕ Ⓖ Ⓗ Ⓙ    **28** Ⓐ Ⓑ Ⓒ Ⓓ    **30** Ⓕ Ⓖ Ⓗ Ⓙ    **31** Ⓐ Ⓑ Ⓒ Ⓓ    **32** Ⓕ Ⓖ Ⓗ Ⓙ

# Test

## Sample A     Sports Cover

Monica likes all kinds of sports. In the fall she plays soccer, and in winter she plays basketball. Spring is the time for baseball. Tennis keeps Monica busy in the summer.

What sport does Monica play in winter?

A   soccer

B   basketball

C   baseball

D   tennis

---

**Directions: Read each selection. Darken the circle for the correct answer to each question, or write your answer in the space provided.**

## Carmen and Sade's Camping Trip

Carmen and Sade jumped out of the van as soon as it pulled into the campsite. The two friends found a perfect spot under a large pine tree to set up their tent. They drove their tent stakes into the ground. Then, after pulling the tent upright and tightening the ropes, the girls placed their sleeping bags inside. Next, they put their food in a plastic bag and hung it from a tree branch to protect it from wild animals. Finally, they chose a safe place to build a fire. They made sure there were neither low branches nor dry grass or leaves near the campfire. They could not wait to show off their work to the others.

1   The friends placed their tent —

   A   next to a lake.

   B   under a pine tree.

   C   near the bathhouse.

   D   far from the road.

2   Why did the campers choose the place for their fire so carefully?

   F   They wanted to be warm.

   G   They wanted to keep the animals away.

   H   They wanted to protect against forest fires.

   J   They wanted to be near the other campers.

3   What is the main idea of the story?

   A   Building a campfire is easy.

   B   Carmen and Sade are friends.

   C   Carmen and Sade set up camp.

   D   Never leave food in the tent.

4   Why is the food hung from a tree?

_____

_____

_____

_____

---

**Answers**

**SA** Ⓐ Ⓑ Ⓒ Ⓓ     **1** Ⓐ Ⓑ Ⓒ Ⓓ     **2** Ⓕ Ⓖ Ⓗ Ⓙ     **3** Ⓐ Ⓑ Ⓒ Ⓓ

# Learning About Kangaroos

Have you ever heard of "roos"? If you lived in Australia, you would know that this word refers to kangaroos. The kangaroo is the national animal of Australia. Its likeness is found on the money, stamps, and national seal of Australia.

The kangaroo belongs to a family known as marsupials. Most female marsupials have pouches in which their young grow and develop. Some marsupials live in New Guinea and on nearby islands, but many live only in Australia. Kangaroos are the largest marsupials.

There are many different kinds of kangaroos. The most common *species* are the red kangaroo and the gray kangaroo. The red kangaroo is the largest species. It lives in the deserts and dry grasslands of central Australia. Gray kangaroos are smaller than the reds. They live in the forests and grasslands of eastern Australia. Wallabies are smaller than kangaroos, and the smallest of all are rat kangaroos. There are more than a hundred million kangaroos in Australia. That means there are six kangaroos for every person in the country.

Kangaroos live in small groups called mobs. A mob is led by a large male called a boomer. There are usually two or three females and their young in a mob. Often other males challenge the boomer for leadership. He chases them off or fights with them.

Let's follow one female gray kangaroo. Five weeks after mating with the boomer, she gives birth to a tiny baby that isn't even an inch long. This *joey* has no hair and cannot see. Only its forearms are strong and ready to use. Strong arms are important because it has to climb up its mother's stomach and into her pouch. If it falls, it will die. Once inside the pouch, it is safe. It will grow larger and develop hair and a strong tail.

When it is about three months old, the joey will first look out of the pouch. About a month later, it will leave the pouch for the first time. It will eat grass and practice hopping. It will stay close to its mother, and at the first sign of danger, dive back into the pouch headfirst.

Eagles and wild dogs sometimes try to kill young kangaroos. Humans are an even greater enemy. Hunters kill thousands of kangaroos every year. The kangaroos watch for enemies as they eat. Kangaroos have good hearing. Each ear can turn in a half circle. When a kangaroo senses danger, it thumps its tail on the ground. Then the mob hops quickly away. Kangaroos can travel thirty miles an hour when they are frightened.

In some parts of Australia there are kangaroo crossing signs. Kangaroos are not careful when they cross roads, and every year thousands of kangaroos are killed by cars. Generally, the Australian government protects kangaroos by passing laws against killing these native animals.

GO ON

**5** In this selection, you can learn—

   **F** about the height and weight of kangaroos.

   **G** about the life of a rat kangaroo.

   **H** why hunters kill kangaroos.

   **J** about the life of a gray kangaroo.

**6** In this selection, the word *joey* means—

   **A** a baby kangaroo.

   **B** a large male kangaroo.

   **C** a young koala bear.

   **D** a native of Australia.

**7** According to the selection, what feature do most female marsupials share?

   **F** tough skin

   **G** long legs

   **H** a pouch

   **J** white fur

**8** Why does a joey stay close to its mother?

_____

_____

_____

_____

_____

_____

_____

**9** According to the selection, what is the first thing a newborn kangaroo does?

   **A** looks out of the pouch

   **B** climbs into its mother's pouch

   **C** tumbles out of the pouch

   **D** opens its eyes

**10** In this selection, the word *species* means—

   **F** an animal that eats only grass.

   **G** a baby animal.

   **H** a kind of animal.

   **J** an enemy.

**11** According to the selection, a boomer chases off other males because—

   **A** he wants to be the leader of the group.

   **B** there isn't enough food for all of them.

   **C** he doesn't like company.

   **D** he is selfish.

**12** Where do red kangaroos live?

   **F** in central Australia

   **G** only in New Guinea

   **H** in eastern Australia

   **J** in western Australia

**13** You would probably find this story in a book called—

   **A** *The Grasslands of Australia.*

   **B** *Taking Care of Your Pet.*

   **C** *Unusual Animals.*

   **D** *Money and Stamps of the World.*

**14** If you wanted to know more about kangaroos, you should—

   **F** travel to Australia.

   **G** read about them in an encyclopedia.

   **H** draw pictures of them.

   **J** visit a pet store.

▶GO ON

# Wilderness Adventure

Carla pulled her jacket closer and looked into the campfire. The night was cold and clear, and even though it was too dark to see them, Carla could smell the pine trees that surrounded the campsite. Thousands of stars sparkled like tiny diamonds in the night sky. It was beautiful! Carla couldn't believe she was actually there in the national park. Just that morning when she woke up in her own bed she thought, "Another hot, humid, boring day, just like every other day this summer."

But then she remembered! Today was different. Her favorite aunt and uncle, Tina and Marc, had invited her to join them on a backpacking trip. They picked her up at 8:00 A.M. and drove most of the day to get to the national park. They just had time to pitch their tents, build the fire, and cook dinner before it got dark. Carla went into the forest to gather firewood. Then she helped Tina make hamburger patties. She didn't realize how hungry she was until she smelled them cooking. Everything tasted better when you were outside, she decided.

"Well, it's too dark to do anything else tonight," Uncle Marc said. "We might as well go to bed now so that we can get up at sunrise. I want to get an early start on the trail. Be sure and zip your tent, Carla. You wouldn't want to wake up with a rattlesnake in your sleeping bag!"

Carla couldn't decide if he was teasing or not. She made sure she zipped the tent tight, just in case. She crawled into her sleeping bag and wiggled around, trying to get comfortable. It had been a long day, but she was too excited to sleep. She wished she had brought a flashlight and a book. She wondered what adventures the next day would bring.

Carla woke up to the sounds of pots clanging. She crawled out of her tent and opened her backpack. "Look at this!" she exclaimed in dismay. Some small creature had chewed a hole in her bag of trail mix and eaten the whole thing. "Well, some little field mouse had a great breakfast!" Tina said. "Never mind, I brought plenty of snacks for all of us."

After breakfast, Carla's uncle helped her adjust her backpack. It was heavier than she expected it to be. Then they took off on the trail. The three hikers followed a river for a while; then they crossed it. Carla held her breath as she walked on the narrow log that served as a bridge. She didn't want to fall into the icy water.

The trail led back into the forest. Tina walked in front, and Carla and Marc followed. Suddenly all three heard a terrifying sound—a loud, close rattle. Tina jumped forward. Carla jumped backwards and bumped into her uncle. About a foot to the right of the trail, they saw what was making the sound—a five-foot-long rattlesnake! The snake continued rattling its tail. They noticed something peculiar about the snake. Its mouth was wide open, and it was eating a field mouse. Apparently the snake was in the middle of its lunch.

Marc relaxed as soon as he realized what was happening. He explained that snakes' teeth point inward. It's very difficult for them to spit something out once they have begun eating. The rattlesnake couldn't harm them as long as it had something in its mouth. Tina got her camera. They sat a short distance away and took pictures while they observed the rattlesnake. The snake continued to rattle but didn't move away. Marc told Carla that snakes eat only every ten days or so. It takes them a long time to swallow and digest their *prey*.

After a while, they left the snake and began hiking again. Carla's heart was still beating fast. She decided that Uncle Marc hadn't been teasing when he told her to zip up her tent. He wouldn't have to remind her about that tonight!

GO ON

**15** The boxes below show events from the selection.

| Carla gathered firewood from the forest. | | Carla walked across the narrow log bridge. |
|---|---|---|
| 1 | 2 | 3 |

Which event belongs in the second box?

A Carla heard a terrifying sound.

B Carla crawled into her sleeping bag.

C Carla watched a rattlesnake eating its prey.

D Carla drove to the national park with her aunt and uncle.

**16** At the beginning of the selection Carla feels—

F angry and disappointed.

G worried and nervous.

H excited and happy.

J lonely and sad.

**17** What is the last thing Carla did before she went to sleep?

A She wiggled around, trying to get comfortable.

B She zipped up the tent.

C She helped Tina make hamburger patties.

D She went looking for rattlesnakes.

**18** Which words in the story show that the evening was cool at the campsite?

F ...zip up her tent.

G ...pulled her jacket closer...

H ...too dark to do anything else...

J ...sparkled like tiny diamonds...

**19** The word *prey* means—

A a kind of snake.

B a type of backpack.

C an animal hunted for food.

D teeth that point inward.

**20** What did the snake most likely do after the three hikers left?

_____

_____

_____

_____

_____

_____

_____

**21** What is this story mainly about?

F summer vacations

G the danger of rattlesnakes

H getting along with relatives

J backpacking in a national park

**22** Why would Uncle Marc not have to remind Carla to zip up her tent at night?

A The snake had frightened her, and she didn't want another one near her.

B She had a good memory and never forgot anything.

C She knew that no one would remind her, so she told herself to remember.

D She didn't want to make her uncle unhappy.

GO ON

Answers

15 Ⓐ Ⓑ Ⓒ Ⓓ    17 Ⓐ Ⓑ Ⓒ Ⓓ    19 Ⓐ Ⓑ Ⓒ Ⓓ    22 Ⓐ Ⓑ Ⓒ Ⓓ

16 Ⓕ Ⓖ Ⓗ Ⓙ    18 Ⓕ Ⓖ Ⓗ Ⓙ    21 Ⓕ Ⓖ Ⓗ Ⓙ

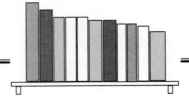

Come to the Read-Over Friday, May 28! It is sponsored by the fourth-grade teachers to kick off the summer reading program. Principal Jones, Ms. Rodriguez, and Coach Lee will also attend. Let's see how many pages fourth graders can read in one night at a sleep-over party!

**Rules and Information**

1. You must be a fourth grader at Main Street School to attend.

2. Get a permission slip from Ms. Barker in Room 211. Have your parents complete the slip and return it by Monday, May 24.

3. Report to the gym at 7:30 P.M. on Friday, May 28, dressed in shorts or jeans and a T-shirt to sleep in.

4. Bring a sleeping bag, pillow, and lots of reading material.

6. We will stay up late and read, read, read!

7. In the morning, we'll tally the total number of pages read.

8. Breakfast will be served at 7:00 A.M.

9. Parents must pick up students by 9:00 A.M. on Saturday, May 29.

**23**  Who can attend the Read-Over?

_____

_____

_____

_____

_____

_____

_____

**24**  Where will students at the Read-Over spend the night?

F   in the principal's office

G   in the library

H   in Room 211

J   in the gym

**25**  Which of these is _not_ important to bring to the Read-Over?

A   sleeping bag

B   reading material

C   flashlight

D   pillow

**26**  When does the Read-Over end?

F   7:30 P.M. on Friday, May 28

G   7:30 A.M. on Friday, May 28

H   7:30 A.M. on Saturday, May 29

J   9:00 A.M. on Saturday, May 29

**27**  Why are the fourth-grade teachers having a Read-Over?

A   to raise money

B   to introduce the summer reading program

C   to help parents

D   to help the librarian

**28**  What is the last date to turn in permission slips?

F   May 12

G   May 13

H   May 24

J   May 5

## Understanding Word Meanings

Directions: Darken the circle for the word or words that have the same or almost the same meaning as the underlined word.

**TRY THIS** Choose your answers carefully. Some choices may seem correct if you do not think about the meaning of the underlined words.

**Sample A**

Peculiar means—

A  tired        C  quick

B  hurt         D  strange

**THINK IT THROUGH** The correct answer is D, strange. Peculiar does not mean "tired," "hurt" or "quick."

1  **Immediately means—**

A  later        C  sadly

B  slowly       D  instantly

2  **Mighty means—**

F  false        H  famous

G  strong       J  soft

3  **To challenge is to—**

A  agree        C  plan

B  dare         D  change

4  **Chilly means—**

F  warm         H  cold

G  nice         J  windy

5  **To dangle means to—**

A  tie          C  catch

B  cover        D  swing

6  **To be scared means to be—**

F  sweaty       H  afraid

G  tired        J  excited

7  **To accuse means to—**

A  honor        C  blame

B  question     D  reward

8  **A slogan is a kind of—**

F  laugh        H  answer

G  motto        J  metal

**Answers**

SA Ⓐ Ⓑ Ⓒ Ⓓ    2 Ⓕ Ⓖ Ⓗ Ⓙ    4 Ⓕ Ⓖ Ⓗ Ⓙ    6 Ⓕ Ⓖ Ⓗ Ⓙ    8 Ⓕ Ⓖ Ⓗ Ⓙ

46   1 Ⓐ Ⓑ Ⓒ Ⓓ    3 Ⓐ Ⓑ Ⓒ Ⓓ    5 Ⓐ Ⓑ Ⓒ Ⓓ    7 Ⓐ Ⓑ Ⓒ Ⓓ

# Matching Words with More Than One Meaning

Directions: Darken the circle for the sentence that uses the underlined word in the same way as the sentence in the box.

**TRY THIS**
Read the sentence in the box carefully. Decide what the underlined word means. Then find the sentence in which the underlined word has the same meaning.

**Sample A**

1
| Did you <u>seal</u> the bag tightly? |

In which sentence does <u>seal</u> have the same meaning as it does in the sentence above?

A   The presidential <u>seal</u> was on the envelope.

B   Matt cared for the baby <u>seal</u>.

C   Break the <u>seal</u>, and open the trunk.

D   We have to <u>seal</u> the cracks in the floor.

**THINK IT THROUGH**

The correct answer is <u>D</u>. In this sentence and in the sentence in the box, <u>seal</u> means to "make secure or fill in."

---

1
| The bus will <u>drop</u> us at the entrance. |

In which sentence does <u>drop</u> have the same meaning as it does in the sentence above?

A   There was one <u>drop</u> of medicine left.

B   Did the bus <u>drop</u> them off at the corner?

C   Business began to <u>drop</u>.

D   She was about to <u>drop</u> the plate.

2
| We stood on the <u>bluff</u> looking at the city. |

In which sentence does <u>bluff</u> have the same meaning as it does in the sentence above?

F   I wanted to call his <u>bluff</u>.

G   They built a house on the wooded <u>bluff</u>.

H   Can you <u>bluff</u> your way out of trouble?

J   Tina recognized the boy's <u>bluff</u>.

3
| Use a hammer to <u>pound</u> the nails. |

In which sentence does <u>pound</u> have the same meaning as it does in the sentence above?

A   I found my dog at the <u>pound</u>.

B   Don't <u>pound</u> your feet on the stairs.

C   <u>Pound</u> this stake into the ground.

D   This weighs more than one <u>pound</u>.

4
| This is my best <u>lace</u> cover. |

In which sentence does <u>lace</u> have the same meaning as it does in the sentence above?

F   My boot <u>lace</u> is torn.

G   Belgian <u>lace</u> is quite beautiful.

H   Would you help Tim <u>lace</u> his boot?

J   Next, <u>lace</u> the ribbons together.

---

**Answers**
**SA** Ⓐ Ⓑ Ⓒ Ⓓ    **1** Ⓐ Ⓑ Ⓒ Ⓓ    **2** Ⓕ Ⓖ Ⓗ Ⓙ    **3** Ⓐ Ⓑ Ⓒ Ⓓ    **4** Ⓕ Ⓖ Ⓗ Ⓙ

# Using Context Clues

**Directions:** Darken the circle for the word or words that give the meaning of the underlined word, or write the answer in the space provided.

> **TRY THIS**
>
> Read the first sentence carefully. Look for clue words in the sentence. Then use each answer choice in place of the underlined word. Remember that the underlined word and your answer must have the same meaning.

**Sample A**

This <u>specific</u> offer is good for only two weeks. **Specific** means—

A  particular          C  radio

B  cheap               D  splendid

> **THINK IT THROUGH**
>
> The correct answer is A. **Specific** means "particular or exact." The clue words are "good for only two weeks." All four choices could describe the offer, but only **particular** has the same meaning as <u>specific</u>.

---

1   The successful athlete has won <u>numerous</u> track awards during her long career. **Numerous** means—

A  many

B  foreign

C  sport

D  secret

2   This <u>pamphlet</u>, published by an environmental group, describes how we can help protect our world. **Pamphlet** means—

F  contest

G  speaker

H  celebration

J  booklet

3   The newest dance is fun, but it has many <u>complicated</u> steps that are hard to remember. **Complicated** means—

A  short

B  divided

C  difficult

D  slow

4   When we asked directions, the man <u>indicated</u> the correct route on our map. **Indicated** means—

F  drove

G  showed

H  left

J  closed

5   The police captain <u>dispatched</u> a rescue team to search for the lost girl. **Dispatched** means—

A  found

B  sent

C  questioned

D  cheered

6   A family finally moved into the house that has been <u>vacant</u> for six months. **Vacant** means—

_____

_____

_____

_____

_____

# Test

**Sample A**

**Drowsy means—**

A  forgetful

B  greedy

C  helpless

D  sleepy

For questions 1–8, darken the circle for the word or words that have the same or almost the same meaning as the underlined word.

**1  Coax means—**

A  sleep

B  hide

C  question

D  persuade

**2  Mammoth means—**

F  dusty

G  shiny

H  huge

J  old

**3  To preserve something is to—**

A  borrow it

B  sell it

C  throw it away

D  save it

**4  To burrow means to—**

F  escape

G  surrender

H  multiply

J  dig

**5  Anxious means—**

A  hopeful

B  glad

C  worried

D  angry

**6  Grave means—**

F  silly

G  serious

H  huge

J  broken

**7  A voyage is a kind of—**

A  store

B  journey

C  cage

D  dance

**8  To disturb means to—**

F  bother

G  sneak

H  disagree

J  ask

Write your answer for the following:

**9  What is an error?**

_____

_____

_____

_____

_____

_____

_____

**GO ON**

**Answers**

SA ⒶⒷⒸⒹ  2 ⒻⒼⒽⒿ  4 ⒻⒼⒽⒿ  6 ⒻⒼⒽⒿ  8 ⒻⒼⒽⒿ

1 ⒶⒷⒸⒹ  3 ⒶⒷⒸⒹ  5 ⒶⒷⒸⒹ  7 ⒶⒷⒸⒹ

49

**Sample B**

> Omar is in the <u>cast</u> of the school play.

In which sentence does <u>cast</u> have the same meaning as it does in the sentence above?

A  We all signed the <u>cast</u> on Dan's arm.

B  Dad can <u>cast</u> his fishing line a long way.

C  We will <u>cast</u> off at noon on Saturday and return Sunday night.

D  They're planning a party for everyone in the <u>cast</u>.

For questions 10–14, darken the circle for the sentence in which the underlined word means the same as it does in the sentence in the box.

**10**
> We are <u>subject</u> to the laws of our state.

In which sentence does <u>subject</u> have the same meaning as it does in the sentence above?

A  What is the <u>subject</u> of the second sentence?

B  Art is Jennifer's favorite <u>subject</u> in school this year.

C  He was a loyal <u>subject</u> of King Phillip.

D  Everyone is <u>subject</u> to catching a cold right now.

**11**
> Can you see the ships in the <u>bay</u>?

In which sentence does <u>bay</u> have the same meaning as it does in the sentence above?

F  Fern likes <u>bay</u> windows.

G  Do wolves <u>bay</u> at the moon?

H  Their house faces the <u>bay</u>.

J  The hero holds his enemies at <u>bay</u>.

**12**
> The stairs had an <u>iron</u> railing.

In which sentence does <u>iron</u> have the same meaning as it does in the sentence above?

A  Do you have to <u>iron</u> this fabric?

B  <u>Iron</u> beams were used in the building.

C  We hope our friends can <u>iron</u> out their differences.

D  Should we buy Mom a new steam <u>iron</u>?

**13**
> Please <u>raise</u> that window.

In which sentence does <u>raise</u> have the same meaning as it does in the sentence above?

F  Did you <u>raise</u> your hand?

G  I <u>raise</u> peppers, carrots, and peas in my garden.

H  How much money did we <u>raise</u> for the community shelter?

J  There's no need to <u>raise</u> your voice.

**14**
> This floor is not <u>level</u>.

In which sentence does <u>level</u> have the same meaning as it does in the sentence above?

A  Please hand me the hammer and the <u>level</u>.

B  You should use one <u>level</u> cup of flour for that recipe.

C  The river rose to a <u>level</u> of twenty feet.

D  He reads on a fifth-grade <u>level</u>.

►GO ON

**Sample C**

Those three people argue and <u>disagree</u> about everything. <u>Disagree</u> means—

A  read

B  sing

C  quarrel

D  plan

🛑 STOP

For questions 15–22, darken the circle for the word or words that give the meaning of the underlined word.

15  The military posted a <u>sentry</u> at the king's door to prevent anyone from entering. A <u>sentry</u> is a—

F  sign

G  crown

H  guard

J  gate

16  Did you fall asleep and <u>neglect</u> to complete your social studies? <u>Neglect</u> means—

A  travel

B  fail

C  argue

D  understand

17  Our newspaper is delivered at 7:00 A.M. <u>daily</u>. <u>Daily</u> means—

F  every day

G  twice a day

H  every week

J  once a month

18  He uses bold, <u>vivid</u> colors in his paintings. <u>Vivid</u> means—

A  mixed

B  soft

C  strong

D  pale

19  This show has an exciting <u>plot</u> that kept us interested. <u>Plot</u> means—

F  hero

G  story

H  writer

J  cast

20  Because conditions were hard, the settlers led a life filled with <u>strife</u>. <u>Strife</u> means—

A  vacation

B  illness

C  struggle

D  religion

21  I couldn't <u>budge</u> the heavy rock. <u>Budge</u> means—

F  buy

G  wash

H  paint

J  move

22  The newborn horse will probably <u>keel</u> over when it tries to stand. <u>Keel</u> means—

A  fall

B  scratch

C  jump

D  run

🛑 STOP

**Answers**

SC Ⓐ Ⓑ Ⓒ Ⓓ    16 Ⓐ Ⓑ Ⓒ Ⓓ    18 Ⓐ Ⓑ Ⓒ Ⓓ    20 Ⓐ Ⓑ Ⓒ Ⓓ    22 Ⓐ Ⓑ Ⓒ Ⓓ

15 Ⓕ Ⓖ Ⓗ Ⓙ    17 Ⓕ Ⓖ Ⓗ Ⓙ    19 Ⓕ Ⓖ Ⓗ Ⓙ    21 Ⓕ Ⓖ Ⓗ Ⓙ

51

# Math: Problem-Solving Strategies

## Overview

### The Problem-Solving Plan

*When solving math problems follow these steps:*

## STEP 1: WHAT IS THE QUESTION/GOAL?

Decide what must be found. This information is usually presented in the form of a question.

## STEP 2: FIND THE FACTS

Locate the factual information in three different ways:

A. KEY FACTS...the facts you need to solve the problem.

B. FACTS YOU DON'T NEED...those facts that are not necessary for solving the problem.

C. ARE MORE FACTS NEEDED?...decide if you have enough information to solve the problem.

## STEP 3: SELECT A STRATEGY

Decide what strategies you might use, how you will use them, and then estimate what your answer will be. If one strategy does not help solve the problem, try another.

## STEP 4: SOLVE

Apply the strategy according to your plan. Use an operation if necessary, and clearly indicate your answer.

## STEP 5: DOES YOUR RESPONSE MAKE SENSE?

Check to make sure that your answer makes sense. Use estimation or approximation strategies.

**PROBLEM/QUESTION:**

Jason has $23.00. Does he have enough money to buy a CD for $14.99 and a cassette tape for $9.99?

**STEP 1: WHAT IS THE QUESTION/GOAL?**

**STEP 2: FIND THE FACTS**

**STEP 3: SELECT A STRATEGY**

**STEP 4: SOLVE**

**STEP 5: DOES YOUR RESPONSE MAKE SENSE?**

## PROBLEM/QUESTION:

Mr. Johnson has 2 twenty dollar bills, 3 ten dollar bills, 4 five dollar bills and 4 one dollar bills. He wants to buy something which costs $38. How can he pay for it with the exact change?

**STEP 1: WHAT IS THE QUESTION/GOAL?**

**STEP 2: FIND THE FACTS**

**STEP 3: SELECT A STRATEGY**

**STEP 4: SOLVE**

**STEP 5: DOES YOUR RESPONSE MAKE SENSE?**

# Math Problem Solving

## Understanding Numeration

**Directions: Darken the circle for the correct answer, or write in the answer.**

| TRY THIS | Read each problem carefully. Be sure to think about which numbers stand for hundreds, tens, and ones. |
| --- | --- |

**Sample A**

What number comes fourth if these numbers are arranged in order from least to greatest?

| 2,345 | 5,423 | 3,254 | 5,234 | 3,542 |
| --- | --- | --- | --- | --- |

A  5,234     C  3,542

B  5,423     D  2,345

| THINK IT THROUGH | The correct answer is A. 2,345 has a 2 in the thousands place and 3,254 has a 3 in the thousands place, as does 3,542. 5,234 comes next, since it has a 5 in the thousands place and a 2 in the hundreds place. The number 5,234 comes fourth. |
| --- | --- |

**STOP**

---

**1** What number means the same as (8 × 1000) + (6 × 100) + (1 × 1)?

A  861       C  8,601

B  80,061    D  8,610

**2** Meiko made this chart of some mountain peaks. Which mountain peak is the shortest?

### Mountain Peaks

| Name | Height (in meters) |
| --- | --- |
| Mount Etna | 3,390 |
| Mount Blanc | 4,807 |
| Mount Fuji | 3,776 |
| Mount Cook | 3,764 |

F  Mount Etna     H  Mount Fuji

G  Mount Blanc    J  Mount Cook

**3** Which words mean 8,902?

A  eighty-nine two

B  eight thousand nine hundred

C  eighty-nine thousand two

D  eight thousand nine hundred two

**4** The school cafeteria offers hamburgers on the menu on even-numbered days during the school week. How many days were hamburgers offered on the menu this month?

| S | M | T | W | T | F | S |
| --- | --- | --- | --- | --- | --- | --- |
|  |  |  |  |  | 1 | 2 |
| 3 | 4 | 5 | 6 | 7 | 8 | 9 |
| 10 | 11 | 12 | 13 | 14 | 15 | 16 |
| 17 | 18 | 19 | 20 | 21 | 22 | 23 |
| 24 | 25 | 26 | 27 | 28 | 29 | 30 |

_____

_____

**STOP**

---

**Answers**

**SA** Ⓐ Ⓑ Ⓒ Ⓓ     **1** Ⓐ Ⓑ Ⓒ Ⓓ     **2** Ⓕ Ⓖ Ⓗ Ⓙ     **3** Ⓐ Ⓑ Ⓒ Ⓓ

# Using Whole Numbers, Fractions, and Decimals

Directions: Darken the circle for the correct answer, or write in the answer.

**TRY THIS** Read the question twice before choosing your answer. Study any pictures given in the problem. Try using all the answer choices back in the problem. Then choose the answer that you think best answers the question.

**Sample A**

Which expression correctly completes the number sentence?

$$6 + 9 = \boxed{\phantom{xxx}}$$

**A** $9 - 6$      **C** $9 + 6$

**B** $15 - 6$      **D** $15 - 9$

**THINK IT THROUGH** The correct answer is <u>C</u>. Numbers may be reversed in addition. The answer will be the same.

---

**1** What fraction tells how many of the dots are shaded in this figure?

**A** $\frac{3}{7}$

**B** $\frac{10}{3}$

**C** $\frac{3}{8}$

**D** $\frac{3}{10}$

**2** What number makes this number sentence true?

$$\boxed{\phantom{x}} \times 1 = 7$$

**F** 8

**G** 7

**H** 6

**J** 5

**3** Which decimal shows the part of the figure that is shaded?

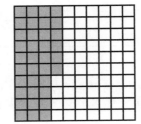

**A** 0.36      **C** 0.34

**B** 0.4      **D** 0.64

**4** What number makes this sentence true?

$$4 + (2 + 3) = (4 + \boxed{\phantom{x}}) + 3$$

_____

_____

_____

**5** Which number sentence is in the same fact family as $3 \times 8 = 24$?

**F** $24 - 8 = 16$

**G** $8 + 3 = 11$

**H** $6 \times 4 = 24$

**J** $24 \div 8 = 3$

---

**Answers**

**SA** Ⓐ Ⓑ Ⓒ Ⓓ     **1** Ⓐ Ⓑ Ⓒ Ⓓ     **2** Ⓕ Ⓖ Ⓗ Ⓙ     **3** Ⓐ Ⓑ Ⓒ Ⓓ     **5** Ⓕ Ⓖ Ⓗ Ⓙ

# Working with Statistics and Probability

Directions: Darken the circle for the correct answer, or write in the answer.

**TRY THIS**

Read the question carefully. Look for key words or numbers in the question that tell you what information to look for in the chart or graph.

## Sample A

Wen is playing a game with the spinner shown here. If it is spun many times, which animal will it probably point to most often?

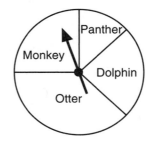

A Dolphin        C Otter

B Panther        D Monkey

**THINK IT THROUGH**

The correct answer is <u>C</u>. The largest section of the spinner is <u>otter</u>. The spinner will probably point to this section most often.

**STOP**

---

The graph below shows some music recordings produced in 1997. Use it to answer questions 1 and 2.

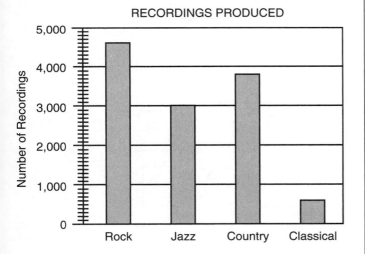

RECORDINGS PRODUCED

1   How many country recordings were produced?

_____

_____

2   How many more rock recordings were produced than jazz recordings?

A 600        C 1,600

B 800        D 4,000

3   The tally chart shows the number of butterflies spotted by four students during one week.

| Name | Number of Butterflies | | | | |
|------|-----|-----|-----|-----|-----|
|      | M | T | W | T | F |
| Dawn | I | IIII | III | ﬤﬤ I | II |
| Del | III | ﬤﬤ III | I | I | ﬤﬤ II |
| Rafael | IIII | II | ﬤﬤ | II | III |
| Kathy | I | ﬤﬤ I | I | III | I |

Who spotted more than 6 butterflies on Tuesday?

F Dawn        H Rafael

G Del         J Kathy

**GO ON**

Answers
SA Ⓐ Ⓑ Ⓒ Ⓓ      2 Ⓐ Ⓑ Ⓒ Ⓓ      3 Ⓕ Ⓖ Ⓗ Ⓙ

The table lists the population of the 6 largest states and the number of members that each state has in the House of Representatives. Study the table. Then use it to answer questions 4 and 5.

| State | Population | Representatives |
|---|---|---|
| California | 29,839,250 | 52 |
| Florida | 13,003,362 | 23 |
| Illinois | 11,466,682 | 20 |
| New York | 18,044,505 | 31 |
| Pennsylvania | 11,964,710 | 21 |
| Texas | 17,059,805 | 30 |

4  Which two states combined have the same number of representatives as California?

_____

_____

_____

_____

5  Which state has more than twice the number of Representatives of Florida?

A  California

B  New York

C  Texas

D  Pennsylvania

6  Terry placed these cubes in a bag. The "G" stands for green, and the "R" stands for red. How often would Terry probably pick a red cube if he reached into the bag without looking?

F  1 out of 9 times

G  1 out of 6 times

H  1 out of 4 times

J  1 out of 3 times

This chart shows the fish tank at a pet store.

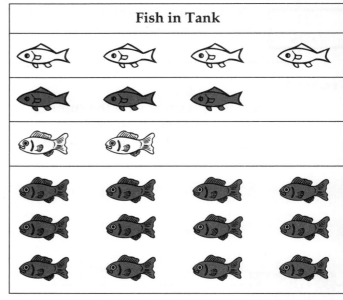

Fish in Tank

7  If the clerk catches a fish in a net, which one will it most likely be?

A

C

B

D

8  Minerva put these shapes into a box. If she reaches into the box and picks one shape, which shape will it most likely be?

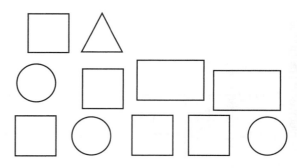

F  a square

G  a triangle

H  a rectangle

J  a circle

STOP

# Understanding Geometry

Directions: Darken the circle for the correct answer, or write in the answer.

**TRY THIS** Read each question carefully. Study the objects named or shown and use them to help you to choose the correct answer.

## Sample A

The graph shows the location of some shapes. What shape is located at (D, 4)?

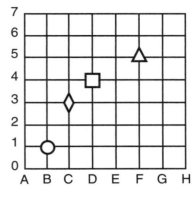

A △          C □

B ○          D ◊

**THINK IT THROUGH** The correct answer is <u>C</u>. To find the location, first go across to D. Next, go up to 4. There is a □ there.

 STOP

---

1   Mona made a card for her mother. If Mona held the card up to a mirror, what would the card look like?

I LOVE YOU

A

C

B

D

2   Which star can be folded on the dotted line so that the two sides match exactly?

F           H

G           J

3   Which names the shape of this traffic sign?

A   octagon

B   hexagon

C   triangle

D   rectangle

GO ON ▶

**Answers**
SA Ⓐ Ⓑ Ⓒ Ⓓ     1 Ⓐ Ⓑ Ⓒ Ⓓ     2 Ⓕ Ⓖ Ⓗ Ⓙ     3 Ⓐ Ⓑ Ⓒ Ⓓ

**4** Which shape has three corners and three sides that are exactly the same?

F    H

G 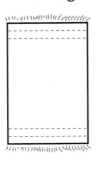   J

**5** What shape is this rug?

_____

_____

_____

**6** Ian is part of the flag patrol. Each day he hangs this flag on the pole.

Today he hung the flag upside down by mistake. What did the flag look like?

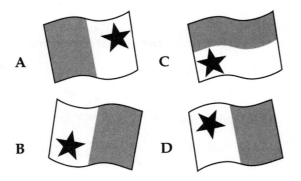

**7** Which letter has more than one line of symmetry?

F  C             H  H

G  W             J  K

**8** Which figure represents a hexagon?

A    C

B             D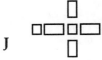

**9** Each set of pieces below fold to form a three-dimensional shape. Which would form a cube?

F             H

G    J

**10** How many corners does this figure have?

_____

_____

_____

_____

STOP

# Working with Measurement

**TRY THIS**

Read each question carefully. Use the objects shown or named to help you answer each question.

## Sample A

Which piece of chalk is the shortest?

A  A

B B

C C

D D

**THINK IT THROUGH**

The correct answer in <u>C</u>. Compare each piece of chalk. Piece <u>C</u> is the shortest.

---

**1** Nancy put some muffins in the oven at the time shown on the clock. They will be ready at 7:20. How many minutes will the muffins take to bake?

A 35 minutes

B 20 minutes

C 15 minutes

D 10 minutes

**2** What is the most likely temperature outside while Gwen shovels snow?

F 68°F      H 55°F

G 32°F      J 82°F

**3** Which figure has the smallest shaded area?

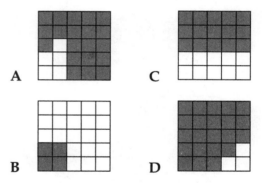

A      C

B      D

**4** Which unit of measurement is best to describe the weight of an egg?

F yards      H inches

G liters      J ounces

---

**GO ON**

**Answers**
SA Ⓐ Ⓑ Ⓒ Ⓓ    **1** Ⓐ Ⓑ Ⓒ Ⓓ    **2** Ⓕ Ⓖ Ⓗ Ⓙ    **3** Ⓐ Ⓑ Ⓒ Ⓓ    **4** Ⓕ Ⓖ Ⓗ Ⓙ

**5** Kerry has these coins.

Which group of coins shows the same value?

**A**

**B**

**C**

**D**

**6** Danny read a book for 30 minutes. He finished reading at 3:00 P.M. Which clock shows the time that he began reading?

**F** | 2:30 P.M. |    **H** | 3:15 P.M. |

**G** | 2:15 P.M. |    **J** | 2:45 P.M. |

**7** Which is most likely to be the length of a bike path?

**A** 25 yards     **C** 25 feet

**B** 25 miles     **D** 25 pounds

**8** Use your centimeter ruler to help you answer this question. How many centimeters long is the trail from the squirrel to the nuts?

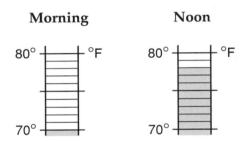

**F** $8\frac{1}{2}$ cm

**G** $10\frac{3}{4}$ cm

**H** $12\frac{1}{2}$ cm

**J** 13 cm

**9** Tim looked at the thermometer in the morning to find out the temperature. He looked again at noon.

Morning                Noon

How does the noon temperature reading differ from the morning temperature?

**A** It is 10° warmer.

**B** It is 10° cooler.

**C** It is 8° warmer.

**D** It is 8° cooler.

STOP

**Answers**
5 Ⓐ Ⓑ Ⓒ Ⓓ     6 Ⓕ Ⓖ Ⓗ Ⓙ     7 Ⓐ Ⓑ Ⓒ Ⓓ     8 Ⓕ Ⓖ Ⓗ Ⓙ     9 Ⓐ Ⓑ Ⓒ Ⓓ

# Understanding Patterns and Relationships

**Directions:** Darken the circle for the correct answer, or write in the answer.

| TRY THIS | Read each question carefully. Look at each answer choice to see which number or figure will answer the question correctly. |

**Sample A**

What comes next in the pattern shown here?

☆ △ ☆ □ ☆ ☾ ☆ △ ☆ ___ ☆

A ☾

B □

C △

D ☆

| THINK IT THROUGH | The correct answer is <u>B</u>. In this pattern, each star is followed by a triangle, a square, or a moon. The missing shape should be the <u>square</u>. |

**STOP**

---

**1** What number completes the pattern in the boxes?

| 52 | 47 | 42 | | 32 | 27 |
|----|----|----|----|----|----|

A   43

B   41

C   37

D   33

**2** The drama class is selling tickets to a play. They group the tickets to keep track of how many tickets each student takes.

| Group | 1 | 2 | 3 | 4 | 5 |
|-------|----|----|----|----|----|
| Tickets | 35 | 40 | | 50 | 55 |

What number is missing for Group 3?

F   41

G   45

H   49

J   56

**3** Mrs. Green is counting cups in the cafeteria. She stacks them into the groups shown on the chart below.

| Stack | 1 | 2 | 3 | 4 | 5 |
|-------|---|----|----|----|---|
| Cups | 8 | 16 | 24 | 32 | |

How many cups will be in Stack 5 if the pattern continues?

A   33

B   38

C   40

D   48

**4** What number completes the pattern in the boxes?

| 48 | 55 | 62 | | 76 | 83 |
|----|----|----|----|----|----|

_____

_____

_____

_____

**STOP**

---

**Answers**
SA Ⓐ Ⓑ Ⓒ Ⓓ     1 Ⓐ Ⓑ Ⓒ Ⓓ     2 Ⓕ Ⓖ Ⓗ Ⓙ     3 Ⓐ Ⓑ Ⓒ Ⓓ

# Estimating

**Directions:** Darken the circle for the correct answer, or write in the answer.

| TRY THIS | Round numbers when you estimate. For some problems, there are no exact answers. Then you should take your best guess. You can check your answer by using the numbers given in the problem. |

**Sample A**

Billy picked 5 baskets of apples in his uncle's orchard. Each basket held *about* 36 apples. Estimate about how many apples Billy picked.

A  100
C  300
B  200
D  500

| THINK IT THROUGH | The correct answer is <u>B</u>. 36 is rounded up to 40. Next, multiply 40 × 5 to estimate how many apples Billy picked. The answer is <u>200</u>. |

**STOP**

---

**1** Mrs. Rogers' Rose Farm had 723 rosebushes. She sold 411 of them. Estimate *about* how many rosebushes Mrs. Rogers had left.

A  100

B  200

C  300

D  400

**2** The school store has 29 boxes of pencils. There are 34 pencils in each box. Estimate *about* how many pencils the school store has.

_____

_____

_____

**3** Ann keeps her sticker collection in special books. If each book holds 12 stickers, estimate *about* how many books she would need to hold 88 stickers.

F  6

G  8

H  9

J  10

**4** The map shows the distances between five cities. Use the map to help you answer this question.

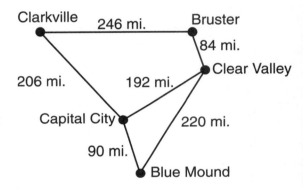

Mr. Tanner wants to drive from Clarkville to Clear Valley using the shortest distance. Estimate *about* how far Mr. Tanner will drive.

A  200 miles

B  300 miles

C  500 miles

D  700 miles

**STOP**

---

Answers
SA Ⓐ Ⓑ Ⓒ Ⓓ    1 Ⓐ Ⓑ Ⓒ Ⓓ    3 Ⓕ Ⓖ Ⓗ Ⓙ    4 Ⓐ Ⓑ Ⓒ Ⓓ

64

# Solving Problems

Directions: Darken the circle for the correct answer, or write in the answer.

 **TRY THIS** Read each question carefully. Look for information in the problem that will help you solve it. Then choose the correct answer.

**Sample A**

Gabriela makes decorative pillows as a hobby. She can sew a pillow in 25 minutes. What additional information is needed to find how long it takes Gabriela to sew an entire set of pillows?

A   The length of each pillow

B   The number of pillows in a set

C   The cost of the materials

D   The number of sets Maria has made

**THINK IT THROUGH** The correct answer is <u>B</u>. Gabriela can sew a pillow in 25 minutes. To find how long it takes her to sew a set of pillows, you must know <u>the number of pillows in a set</u>. This number is multiplied by 25 minutes per pillow.

STOP

---

1   Julio can save $12 a week from his allowance and paper route. Which number sentence shows how to find the amount that he will have saved in 6 weeks?

A   $12 \times 6 = \square$

B   $12 - 6 = \square$

C   $6 + \square = 12$

D   $12 \div 6 = \square$

2   Frank likes hamburgers better than hot dogs. He likes peanut butter less than hot dogs. He prefers pizza to hamburgers. Which food is his favorite?

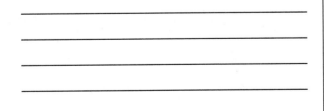

3   What number is inside the triangle, outside the square, and is an even number?

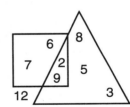

F   3

G   5

H   8

J   12

4   The library placed 8 new videotapes on each shelf of the display case. There are 4 shelves in the case. Which number sentence shows how to find the number of new tapes in the display case?

A   $8 \div 4 = \square$

B   $8 + 4 = \square$

C   $8 - 4 = \square$

D   $8 \times 4 = \square$

 STOP

---

**Answers**
SA Ⓐ Ⓑ Ⓒ Ⓓ   1 Ⓐ Ⓑ Ⓒ Ⓓ   3 Ⓕ Ⓖ Ⓗ Ⓙ   4 Ⓐ Ⓑ Ⓒ Ⓓ

# Math Procedures
## Using Computation

Directions: Darken the circle for the correct answer. Darken the circle for *NH, Not Here,* if the answer is not given. If no choices are given, write in the answer.

| TRY THIS | Study each problem carefully. Decide if you should add, subtract, multiply, or divide. Then work the problem on scratch paper. Be sure to line up the digits. Remember to regroup where necessary. |
|---|---|

**Sample A**

$$59 \times 33$$

A  19,470
B  3,340
C  1,947
D  334
E  NH

| THINK IT THROUGH | The correct answer is <u>C</u>. When you multiply 59 by 33, the answer is <u>1,947</u>. You can check this by multiplying 33 by 59. You should get the same answer. |
|---|---|

STOP

---

**1**

$7 \times \square = 49$

A  0
B  6
C  42
D  56
E  NH

**2**

$$722 - 39$$

_____
_____
_____
_____

**3**

$184 + 767 + 302 = \square$

F  1,353
G  1,253
H  1,243
J  1,153
K  NH

**4**

$63 \div 9 =$

A  4
B  5
C  6
D  7
E  NH

**5**

$6\overline{)18}$

F  24
G  12
H  3
J  2
K  NH

**6**

$$32 \times 6$$

A  192
B  182
C  98
D  38
E  NH

STOP

**Answers**
SA Ⓐ Ⓑ Ⓒ Ⓓ Ⓔ       3 Ⓕ Ⓖ Ⓗ Ⓙ Ⓚ       5 Ⓕ Ⓖ Ⓗ Ⓙ Ⓚ
66   1 Ⓐ Ⓑ Ⓒ Ⓓ Ⓔ       4 Ⓐ Ⓑ Ⓒ Ⓓ Ⓔ       6 Ⓐ Ⓑ Ⓒ Ⓓ Ⓔ

# Using Computation in Context

Directions: Darken the circle for the correct answer. Darken the circle for *NH, Not Here,* if the answer is not given.

> **TRY THIS**
>
> Read each problem carefully. Decide if you need to round, add, subtract, multiply, or divide the numbers. Think about which numbers stand for ones, tens, and hundreds. Work the problem on scratch paper. Remember to regroup where necessary.

**Sample A**

Great Meadow Elementary has 1,058 students. *About* how many students are there if the number is rounded to the nearest ten?

A  1,100
B  1,060
C  1,050
D  6,0
E  NH

> **THINK IT THROUGH**
>
> The correct answer is <u>B</u>. When rounding to the nearest 10, look at the number in the ones column. If it is greater than 4, round up. 1,058 is rounded to <u>1,060</u>.

---

**1** Wanda has 16 compact disks of rock music and 8 compact disks of country music. How many compact disks does Wanda have altogether?

A  2
B  3
C  8
D  24
E  NH

**2** It took Sue 45 minutes to do her homework. She spent 22 minutes working math problems and 10 minutes answering science questions. The remaining time she read. How many minutes did Sue read?

F  35
G  32
H  23
J  13
K  NH

**3** Sam is reading a book with 194 pages. He reads 83 pages.

How many pages does he have left to read?

A  101
B  110
C  111
D  121
E  NH

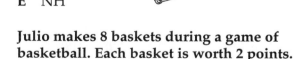

**4** Julio makes 8 baskets during a game of basketball. Each basket is worth 2 points.

How many points did Julio score during the game?

F  6
G  10
H  15
J  18
K  NH

---

**Answers**
**SA** Ⓐ Ⓑ Ⓒ Ⓓ Ⓔ     **2** Ⓕ Ⓖ Ⓗ Ⓙ Ⓚ     **4** Ⓕ Ⓖ Ⓗ Ⓙ Ⓚ
**1** Ⓐ Ⓑ Ⓒ Ⓓ Ⓔ     **3** Ⓐ Ⓑ Ⓒ Ⓓ Ⓔ

# Test

## Sample A

$$\begin{array}{r} 43 \\ \times\, 6 \end{array}$$

A 109
B 248
C 258
D 259
E NH

**STOP**

## Sample B

Sonia used 32 blocks to build a castle. She used 12 rectangles and 15 squares. The other blocks were triangles.

How many triangles did Sonia use to build a castle?

F 27
G 17
H 5
J 3
K NH

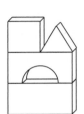

**STOP**

For questions 1–22, darken the circle for the correct answer. Darken the circle for *NH, Not Here,* if the correct answer is not given, or write in the answer.

**1**

20)340

A 170
B 120
C 17
D 12
E NH

**2**

$$\begin{array}{r} 257 \\ \times\, 4 \end{array}$$

F 1,121
G 1,191
H 1,091
J 1,021
K NH

**3**

$56 \div 7 = \square$

A 6
B 7
C 8
D 9
E NH

**4**

$$\begin{array}{r} 426 \\ -\, 52 \end{array}$$

_____
_____
_____
_____

**5**

$5 \times 4 = \square$

F 1
G 9
H 15
J 25
K NH

**6**

5)67

A 14
B 13 R2
C 13
D 11 R4
E NH

**7**

$$\begin{array}{r} 400 \\ -\, 139 \end{array}$$

F 261
G 339
H 371
J 539
K NH

**8**

$$\begin{array}{r} 50 \\ \times\, 30 \end{array}$$

A 1,500
B 1,050
C 1,015
D 150
E NH

**GO ON**

## Answers

SA Ⓐ Ⓑ Ⓒ Ⓓ Ⓔ
SB Ⓕ Ⓖ Ⓗ Ⓙ Ⓚ
1 Ⓐ Ⓑ Ⓒ Ⓓ Ⓔ

2 Ⓕ Ⓖ Ⓗ Ⓙ Ⓚ
3 Ⓐ Ⓑ Ⓒ Ⓓ Ⓔ
5 Ⓕ Ⓖ Ⓗ Ⓙ Ⓚ

6 Ⓐ Ⓑ Ⓒ Ⓓ Ⓔ
7 Ⓕ Ⓖ Ⓗ Ⓙ Ⓚ
8 Ⓐ Ⓑ Ⓒ Ⓓ Ⓔ

**9**

$750 + 228 + 56 = \square$

F  924

G  934

H  1,024

J  1,034

K  NH

**10**  Chou has $10.00. She buys lunch for $5.23, including tax.

How much money will Chou have left?

_____

_____

_____

_____

**11**  Melissa buys these school supplies.

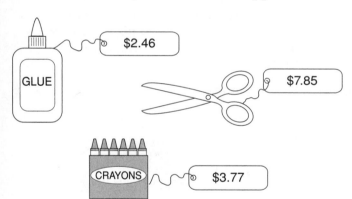

GLUE  $2.46

$7.85

CRAYONS  $3.77

How much will these three items cost altogether before tax is added?

A  $15.08

B  $14.08

C  $12.98

D  $12.08

E  NH

**12**  Coach Reid orders a case of 450 baseball caps. He gives out 231 caps the first week.

How many caps are left?

F  119

G  129

H  219

J  229

K  NH

**13**  A box of popcorn costs 5 tickets at the school fair. Bill buys 7 boxes of popcorn for himself and his 6 cousins.

How many tickets did Bill use to buy the popcorn?

A  12

B  22

C  35

D  40

E  NH

**14**  The librarian ordered 1,236 books last year. *About* how many books were ordered if that number is rounded to the nearest hundred?

F  1,000

G  1,200

H  1,240

J  1,300

K  NH

**15**  Marlon bought a coat for $37.88. *About* how much did Marlon spend if that amount is rounded to the nearest dollar?

A  $37.00

B  $37.90

C  $38.00

D  $40.00

E  NH

GO ON

**16** Mrs. Samuels buys 18 buttons. She has 2 shirts, and she puts the same number of buttons on each shirt.

How many buttons will Mrs. Samuels put on each shirt?

F   6

G   9

H   10

J   12

K   NH

**17** Mrs. Maldonado sells 62 calculators in one week. Each calculator costs $4.

How much money did Mrs. Maldonado make selling the calculators?

A   $258

B   $256

C   $248

D   $246

E   NH

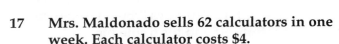

**18** Ed had to pack empty soda bottles for the recycling center. Each box holds 8 bottles.

How many boxes will Ed need to pack 72 bottles?

F   8

G   7

H   6

J   5

K   NH

**19** A toy company has 57 wagons that need wheels.

If 4 wheels are put on each wagon, how many wheels will the toy company use?

A   228

B   224

C   208

D   204

E   NH

**20** Jim is making a birdhouse. He has a board that is 37 inches long. He cuts a piece that is 7 inches long for the roof.

If Jim cuts the rest of the board into 5 equal pieces to make the sides and floor of the birdhouse, how long will each piece be?

_____

_____

_____

_____

_____

**21** Kyra's dog weighs 115 pounds. Her brother's dog weighs 42 pounds. How much heavier is Kyra's dog than her brother's dog?

F   73 pounds

G   83 pounds

H   157 pounds

J   167 pounds

K   NH

**22** The pet store has 16 fish. The owner decides to sell 3 fish for the price of 1.

If people buy 3 fish each time, how many extra fish will be left?

A   0

B   1

C   2

D   3

E   NH

# Test

## Sample A

What number makes the number sentence true?

$$5 + (2 + \square) = (5 + 2) + 6$$

A 2

B 5

C 6

D 7

---

For questions 1–36, darken the circle for the correct answer, or write in the answer.

**1** A museum recorded the number of people visiting in one week. Which day had the largest number of visitors?

| Museum Attendance | |
|---|---|
| Sunday | 4,198 |
| Monday | 2,797 |
| Tuesday | 2,143 |
| Wednesday | 3,033 |
| Thursday | 3,419 |
| Friday | 3,851 |
| Saturday | 4,382 |

A Sunday

B Thursday

C Friday

D Saturday

**2** What number means the same as $(2 \times 1,000) + (7 \times 10) + (8 \times 1)$?

F 278

G 2,078

H 2,708

J 8,680

**3** Jamal sold 3,460 raffle tickets. Write this number in words.

_____

_____

_____

**4** Which expression will correctly complete the number sentence?

$$4 + 8 = \boxed{\phantom{xxxxx}}$$

A $12 + 4$

B $8 \times 4$

C $8 - 4$

D $8 + 4$

**5** Which number has a four in the thousands place and a three in the tens place?

F 4,631

G 3,461

H 4,384

J 2,430

**6** Which two numbers make the sentence correct?

$$(3 + \square) + 5 = (\square + 7) + 4$$

A 5 and 2

B 3 and 1

C 2 and 1

D 5 and 3

**7** Which number sentence is in the same fact family as $5 \times 4 = 20$?

F $5 + 4 = 9$

G $20 \div 4 = 5$

H $20 - 9 = 11$

J $10 \times 2 = 20$

>GO ON

**8** Which mixed number tells what part of the figures are shaded?

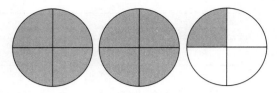

A $2\frac{3}{4}$

B 3

C $2\frac{1}{3}$

D $2\frac{1}{4}$

**9** Students in Mrs. Ford's class are reading a book. Mike has read $\frac{2}{7}$ of the book, Ling has read $\frac{5}{6}$ of the book, Dikim has read $\frac{1}{5}$ of the book, and Artez has read $\frac{3}{4}$ of the book. How would these amounts be listed in order from most to least?

F $\frac{5}{6}, \frac{3}{4}, \frac{2}{7}, \frac{1}{5}$

G $\frac{3}{4}, \frac{1}{5}, \frac{5}{6}, \frac{2}{7}$

H $\frac{1}{5}, \frac{2}{7}, \frac{3}{4}, \frac{5}{6}$

J $\frac{5}{6}, \frac{2}{7}, \frac{3}{4}, \frac{1}{5}$

**10** Which decimal tells the part of the figure that is shaded?

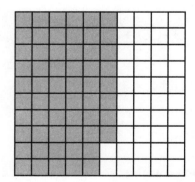

A 0.43

B 0.58

C 0.42

D 0.60

**11** Martha records the weight of four puppies.

| Puppy | Weight |
|-------|--------|
| Red | 19.23 pounds |
| Spot | 20.09 pounds |
| Chico | 12.76 pounds |
| Buster | 15.42 pounds |

Which dog's weight shows a two in the tenths place?

_____

_____

_____

_____

**12** Which figure is $\frac{2}{3}$ shaded?

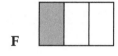

F

G

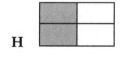

H

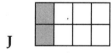

J

**13** After picking berries, three children compared the amounts in their buckets. Luis' bucket was $\frac{2}{3}$ full, Elisa's bucket was $\frac{4}{5}$ full, and Lillian's bucket was $\frac{3}{8}$ full. How would the amounts be arranged if they were ordered from least to most?

A $\frac{3}{8}, \frac{4}{5}, \frac{2}{3}$

B $\frac{2}{3}, \frac{3}{8}, \frac{4}{5}$

C $\frac{3}{8}, \frac{2}{3}, \frac{4}{5}$

D $\frac{4}{5}, \frac{2}{3}, \frac{3}{8}$

GO ON

**Answers**

**8** Ⓐ Ⓑ Ⓒ Ⓓ    **9** Ⓕ Ⓖ Ⓗ Ⓙ    **10** Ⓐ Ⓑ Ⓒ Ⓓ    **12** Ⓕ Ⓖ Ⓗ Ⓙ    **13** Ⓐ Ⓑ Ⓒ Ⓓ

This chart shows the number of days spent in each city by the Smith family on their vacation to Florida. Use the chart to answer questions 14 and 15.

| City | Number of Days |
|---|---|
| Miami | III |
| Ft. Lauderdale | II |
| Orlando | ʘʘ III |
| Tampa | IIII |
| Naples | ʘʘ |

**14** In how many cities did the Smith family spend more than 3 days?

F 2

G 3

H 4

J 5

**15** How many more days did the Smith family spend in Orlando than in Naples?

A 3

B 10

C 13

D 14

**16** If you spin the spinner many times, which number will the spinner point to most often?

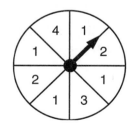

F 1

G 2

H 3

J 4

The graph shows the results of a survey taken at the mall about the desserts most people like. Use the graph to answer questions 17–19.

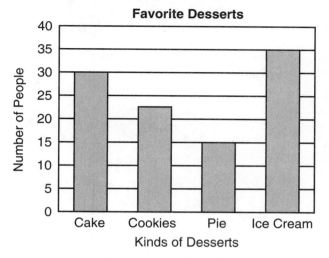

**17** How many more people liked ice cream than pie?

A 50

B 40

C 30

D 20

**18** What total number of people liked cake?

F 15

G 30

H 35

J 40

**19** Which dessert was the least favorite?

_____

_____

_____

_____

▶GO ON▶

**Answers**
**14** Ⓕ Ⓖ Ⓗ Ⓙ    **15** Ⓐ Ⓑ Ⓒ Ⓓ    **16** Ⓕ Ⓖ Ⓗ Ⓙ    **17** Ⓐ Ⓑ Ⓒ Ⓓ    **18** Ⓕ Ⓖ Ⓗ Ⓙ

**20** Jessica has these coins.

**Which group of coins shows the same value?**

**A**

**B**

**C**

**D**

**21** The graph shows the location of some fruit. What fruit is located at (C, 5)?

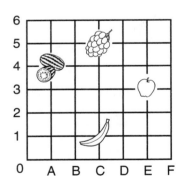

**F** watermelon

**G** banana

**H** grapes

**J** apple

**22** Ruth has this bill. She buys the baseball.

**How much change will Ruth get back?**

**A** 47¢          **C** 66¢

**B** 57¢          **D** 67¢

**23** What shape is the envelope?

**24** Look at the angles labeled A, B, and C on the figure shown here.

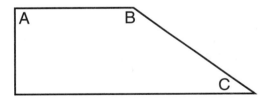

**Which angle shown in the answer choices matches the angle for letter B?**

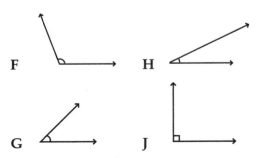

---

**Answers**

GO ON

**25** The clock shows the time Alex finished mowing the lawn. It took him 50 minutes. At what time did he begin mowing the lawn?

A 2:30

B 3:00

C 3:15

D 4:00

**26** Which chain is the longest?

**27** Use your centimeter ruler to help you answer this question. How long is the piggy bank from the snout to the tail?

_____

_____

_____

_____

**28** Mel decided to take a walk in the woods. He looked at the thermometer before he left. Mel looked at the thermometer again when he returned from his walk.

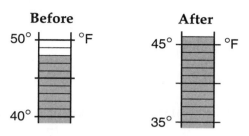

What is the difference in the temperature from the time before and after Mel took his walk?

A  2° warmer        C  12° warmer

B  2° cooler         D  12° cooler

**29** What is the missing number that completes the pattern in the boxes?

| 101 | 104 | 107 | | 113 | 116 |
|-----|-----|-----|-----|-----|-----|

F  117        H  112

G  114        J  110

**30** Use your inch ruler. What is the distance from point A to point B?

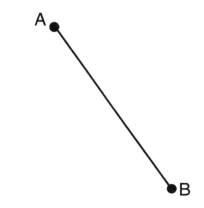

A  1 inch        C  3 inches

B  2 inches      D  4 inches

GO ON

**Answers**
**25** Ⓐ Ⓑ Ⓒ Ⓓ    **26** Ⓕ Ⓖ Ⓗ Ⓙ    **28** Ⓐ Ⓑ Ⓒ Ⓓ    **29** Ⓕ Ⓖ Ⓗ Ⓙ    **30** Ⓐ Ⓑ Ⓒ Ⓓ

**31** The cost of some software is between $60 and $70. The sum of the digits is 18. Which amount could be the price of the software?

F $57.80

G $60.78

H $66.60

J $76.50

**32** The population of Alaska in the 1990 census was 525,000. What other information do you need to have to determine how this state's population compares with the population of Hawaii?

A The population of Hawaii

B The state with the largest population

C The state with the smallest population

D The population of California

**33** Which number is greater than 10, less than 15, and is not inside the circle?

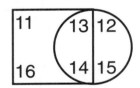

F 11

G 12

H 13

J 16

**34** The movie theater has 325 seats. The ticket seller has already sold 186 tickets. Estimate *about* how many seats are left in the theater.

A 100

B 200

C 400

D 500

**35** Ms. Fernandez is making a quilt. The chart shows the number of triangles she cuts and groups together to make a square.

| Square | 1 | 2 | 3 | 4 | 5 |
|---|---|---|---|---|---|
| Number of Triangles | 12 | 20 | 28 | 36 | |

How many triangles will be in Square 5 if the pattern continues?

_____

_____

_____

_____

**36** Ms. Kwon works in the school cafeteria. She has 138 cartons of milk that need to be stacked on the refrigerator shelf. She can fit 14 cartons in a row. Estimate *about* how many rows of milk cartons Ms. Kwon can make.

F 2

G 10

H 50

J 100

## Listening for Word Meanings

**Directions:** Darken the circle for the word or words that best complete the sentence you hear.

> **TRY THIS**
>
> Listen carefully to the sentence. Then look at the answer choices. If you have difficulty finding the correct word, decide which words you know are wrong. Then look at the remaining words to make your choice.

**Sample A**

    **A** difficult

    **B** polished

    **C** funny

    **D** frightening

> **THINK IT THROUGH**
>
> The correct answer is <u>C</u>, <u>funny</u>. Something that is amusing is not difficult, polished, or frightening. Something that is amusing is <u>funny</u>.

STOP

---

**1**
  **A** make smaller     **C** make better
  **B** make larger     **D** make worse

**2**
  **F** a plan     **H** an area
  **G** a ruler     **J** a village

**3**
  **A** house     **C** dance
  **B** car     **D** boat

**4**
  **F** song for two     **H** role for a child
  **G** carnival for many     **J** game for three

**5**
  **A** real     **C** false
  **B** valuable     **D** decorated

**6**
  **F** feast     **H** concert
  **G** meeting     **J** wedding

**7**
  **A** dodge it     **C** think about it
  **B** welcome it     **D** reward it

**8**
  **F** ordinary     **H** skillful
  **G** familiar     **J** elementary

**9**
  **A** receive it     **C** clean it
  **B** sell it     **D** trade it

**10**
  **F** story     **H** person
  **G** place     **J** plan

STOP

---

**Answers**

**SA** Ⓐ Ⓑ Ⓒ Ⓓ     **3** Ⓐ Ⓑ Ⓒ Ⓓ     **6** Ⓕ Ⓖ Ⓗ Ⓙ     **9** Ⓐ Ⓑ Ⓒ Ⓓ

  **1** Ⓐ Ⓑ Ⓒ Ⓓ     **4** Ⓕ Ⓖ Ⓗ Ⓙ     **7** Ⓐ Ⓑ Ⓒ Ⓓ     **10** Ⓕ Ⓖ Ⓗ Ⓙ

  **2** Ⓕ Ⓖ Ⓗ Ⓙ     **5** Ⓐ Ⓑ Ⓒ Ⓓ     **8** Ⓕ Ⓖ Ⓗ Ⓙ

# Building Listening Skills

Directions: Darken the circle for the word or words that best answer the question.

---

**TRY THIS**  Form a picture of the story in your mind. Listen carefully for details given in the story.

**Sample A**

  A  grass

  B  cotton

  C  silk

  D  wool

**THINK IT THROUGH**  The correct answer is <u>C</u>, <u>silk</u>. The story says that spiders use silk thread to spin webs.

STOP

---

1  A  huge          C  friendly

   B  warm          D  small

2  F  whales        H  dinosaurs

   G  horses        J  elephants

3  A  the mall

   B  the grocery store

   C  her school

   D  the library

4  F  six           H  three

   G  two           J  four

5  A  complain about lost pencils

   B  get you to go to a grocery store

   C  sell you a product

   D  tell how pencils are made

6  F  It is a No. 2 pencil.

   G  It is easy to keep track of.

   H  You'll love it.

   J  It is special.

7  A  at a grocery store

   B  at a hardware store

   C  at a pet store

   D  at a convenience store

8  F  You can buy it at a grocery store.

   G  It is a No. 2 pencil.

   H  It is easier to write with.

   J  It has an adhesive backing.

9  A  8 out of 10      C  9 out of 10

   B  5 out of 10      D  10 out of 10

10  F  Metro Creek     H  the exit

    G  soccer fields   J  the playground

11  A  a picnic area   C  tennis courts

    B  a playground    D  soccer fields

12  F  how to get to City Park from downtown

    G  how to get from the entrance of City Park to the picnic area

    H  how to get to the local lake

    J  how to get to the new golf course

STOP

---

**Answers**

SA  Ⓐ Ⓑ Ⓒ Ⓓ      3  Ⓐ Ⓑ Ⓒ Ⓓ      6  Ⓕ Ⓖ Ⓗ Ⓙ      9  Ⓐ Ⓑ Ⓒ Ⓓ      12  Ⓕ Ⓖ Ⓗ Ⓙ

1  Ⓐ Ⓑ Ⓒ Ⓓ      4  Ⓕ Ⓖ Ⓗ Ⓙ      7  Ⓐ Ⓑ Ⓒ Ⓓ      10  Ⓕ Ⓖ Ⓗ Ⓙ

2  Ⓕ Ⓖ Ⓗ Ⓙ      5  Ⓐ Ⓑ Ⓒ Ⓓ      8  Ⓕ Ⓖ Ⓗ Ⓙ      11  Ⓐ Ⓑ Ⓒ Ⓓ

# Test

**Sample A**

    **A** address     **C** entrance hall

    **B** dining hall     **D** kitchen

**For questions 1–13, darken the circle for the word or words that best complete the sentence you hear.**

**1**
- **A** amaze
- **B** receive
- **C** work
- **D** push

**2**
- **F** give away
- **G** stumble over
- **H** take by force
- **J** find out

**3**
- **A** new
- **B** easy
- **C** dangerous
- **D** childish

**4**
- **F** surprise
- **G** remember
- **H** frighten
- **J** forget

**5**
- **A** trees
- **B** animals
- **C** people
- **D** flowers

**6**
- **F** loudly
- **G** unclearly
- **H** slowly
- **J** quickly

**7**
- **A** again
- **B** under
- **C** hardly
- **D** almost

**8**
- **F** small bite
- **G** fresh piece
- **H** large slice
- **J** spoiled part

**9**
- **A** shiny
- **B** slick
- **C** soft
- **D** small

**10**
- **F** sell it
- **G** like it
- **H** hide it
- **J** lose it

**11**
- **A** crust
- **B** center
- **C** size
- **D** color

**12**
- **F** suggest it
- **G** write it
- **H** show it
- **J** bury it

**13**
- **A** tired
- **B** foolish
- **C** clever
- **D** guilty

**Answers**

**SA** (A) (B) (C) (D)    **3** (A) (B) (C) (D)    **6** (F) (G) (H) (J)    **9** (A) (B) (C) (D)    **12** (F) (G) (H) (J)

**1** (A) (B) (C) (D)    **4** (F) (G) (H) (J)    **7** (A) (B) (C) (D)    **10** (F) (G) (H) (J)    **13** (A) (B) (C) (D)

**2** (F) (G) (H) (J)    **5** (A) (B) (C) (D)    **8** (F) (G) (H) (J)    **11** (A) (B) (C) (D)

79

**Sample B**

    **A**  two hundred dollars

    **B**  twenty dollars

    **C**  one hundred dollars

    **D**  fifty dollars

————————————————

**For questions 14–25, listen to the story. Then darken the circle for the word or words that best answer the question.**

**14**   **F**  keep people from using the pool

      **G**  keep people safe at the pool

      **H**  keep people from having fun at the pool

      **J**  keep the pool from getting crowded

**15**   **A**  talking

      **B**  running

      **C**  diving

      **D**  laughing

**16**   **F**  glass containers

      **G**  children

      **H**  picnic baskets

      **J**  plastic containers

**17**   **A**  sunglasses

      **B**  buttons

      **C**  a scarf

      **D**  a hat

**18**   **F**  happy

      **G**  curious

      **H**  excited

      **J**  sad

**19**   **A**  grew

      **B**  melted

      **C**  talked

      **D**  fell

**20**   **F**  "A Winter Day"

      **G**  "How to Make a Snowman"

      **H**  "Spring Is Coming"

      **J**  "Josh and His Snowman"

**21**   **A**  summer and fall

      **B**  spring and summer

      **C**  fall and winter

      **D**  winter and spring

**22**   **F**  35 miles an hour

      **G**  50 miles an hour

      **H**  75 miles an hour

      **J**  100 miles an hour

**23**   **A**  states along the Great Lakes

      **B**  states along the Mississippi River

      **C**  states along the Atlantic Ocean

      **D**  all states

**24**   **F**  cool ocean water

      **G**  warm ocean water

      **H**  cool land

      **J**  warm land

**25**   **A**  tell a story about hurricanes

      **B**  describe famous hurricanes

      **C**  give information about hurricanes

      **D**  teach hurricane safety

STOP

## Prewriting, Composing, and Editing

**Directions:** Read each sentence carefully. Then darken the circle for the correct answer to each question, or write in the answer.

| TRY THIS | Pretend that you are writing each sentence. Use the rules you have learned for capitalization, punctuation, word usage, and sentence structure to choose the correct answer. |

**Sample A**

### Stormy Weather

Loretta is a member of her town's baseball team. She looks forward to her baseball games, but many times the games are canceled because of bad weather. Loretta became interested in what causes storms. So when her class was studying about weather, Loretta was eager to do a report on the subject.

Which of these topics should *not* be included in Loretta's report?

A   the causes of rain

B   how the sun affects weather

C   vacation places with good weather

D   how thunderstorms are created

| THINK IT THROUGH | The correct answer is C. Loretta is interested in the causes of storms. Choices A, B, and D are about this topic. Choice C, vacation places with good weather, is not about this topic. |

**STOP**

### Humans on the Moon

Cliff is very interested in outer space. His science class is studying the solar system, and this week they learned about the moon. Cliff had to summarize what he learned in a paragraph.

Human beings cannot live on the moon
**(1)**
today. For one thing, there is no air or water
**(2)**
on the moon. Also, the moon's climate is
**(3)**
very extreme. The first time people walked
**(4)**
on the moon was in 1969. The days are
**(5)**
boiling hot, and the nights are freezing cold.

1   Which sentence does *not* belong in this paragraph?

A   1

B   2

C   3

D   4

**GO ON**

**Answers**
SA Ⓐ Ⓑ Ⓒ Ⓓ    1 Ⓐ Ⓑ Ⓒ Ⓓ

Loretta needed to use the dictionary to look up some words to use in her report.

barometer

forecast

sleet

precipitation

**2**  How can these words be changed so that they are in alphabetical (ABC) order?

    **F**  put <u>barometer</u> after <u>forecast</u>

    **G**  put <u>sleet</u> before <u>forecast</u>

    **H**  put <u>precipitation</u> first

    **J**  put <u>sleet</u> after <u>precipitation</u>

**3**  Which guide words might mark the page on which Loretta would find the word *hail*?

    **A**  haddock–halibut

    **B**  Halloween–hammer

    **C**  hangar–harbor

    **D**  hardly–harness

Study this Index from a book Loretta found about weather. Then answer questions 4–7.

---

### Index

air pressure, 90–92
clouds
    cirrus, 51
    cumulus, 52
    stratus, 48
hail, 61–63
hurricane, 74–76
lightning, 66–70
rain, 54–64
sleet, 61–64
tornado, 70–72
weather forecasting, 106–108

---

**4**  On what pages could Loretta find out how weather is forecast?

_____

_____

_____

_____

_____

_____

**5**  All of these pages would have information about clouds *except*—

    **F**  48        **H**  52

    **G**  51        **J**  90

**6**  Which page would probably have information about the causes of tornadoes?

    **A**  55        **C**  71

    **B**  62        **D**  75

**7**  Which page would have information about lightning?

    **F**  51        **H**  71

    **G**  67        **J**  75

**GO ON**

**Answers**

  **2** Ⓕ Ⓖ Ⓗ Ⓙ    **3** Ⓐ Ⓑ Ⓒ Ⓓ    **5** Ⓕ Ⓖ Ⓗ Ⓙ    **6** Ⓐ Ⓑ Ⓒ Ⓓ    **7** Ⓕ Ⓖ Ⓗ Ⓙ

**Here is a rough draft of the first part of Loretta's report. Read the rough draft carefully. Then answer questions 8–14.**

## Understanding the Weather

Did you ever notice how much about the weather people talk? That's
**(1)**                                                          **(2)**

probably because much of what we do depends on the weather. A rainy
**(3)**

day can ruin a picnic. On a cold day a car can have trouble starting
**(4)**

because of the cold.

To find out what kind of weather you're going to have, you could
**(5)**

listen to a weather report. The weather report will tell you about a few
**(6)**

things. One thing it will tell you is the temperature this is how hot or
**(7)**

cold the air is. Another thing it will tell you is whether there will be
**(8)**

any precipitation. Such as rain or snow. About the wind is the third
**(9)**                              **(10)**

thing that a weather report will tell you. It will tell you how hard the
**(11)**

wind is blowing. It will tell you from which direction it is coming.
**(12)**

Knowing what the temperature, the precipitation, and the winds are
**(13)**

like will give you a good idea about the weather for the day.

**8** What is the best way to write sentence 1?

   **A** Did you ever notice about the weather how much people talk?

   **B** Did you ever notice how much people talk about the weather?

   **C** Did you ever notice how much people about the weather talk?

   **D** As it is written.

**9** The best way to write sentence 3 is—

   **F** By a rainy day, a picnic can be ruined.

   **G** A picnic by a rainy day can be ruined.

   **H** A rainy day a picnic can ruin.

   **J** As it is written.

**10** Which sentence could be added after sentence 4?

   **A** About 44,000 storms occur in the world every day.

   **B** Some parts of the United States have very little rain.

   **C** A storm can cancel a baseball game.

   **D** A person who studies the weather is a meteorologist.

**11** Which sentence needlessly repeats a word or group of words?

   **F** 4

   **G** 6

   **H** 8

   **J** 13

**12** What is the best way to write sentence 7?

   **A** One thing it will tell you is the temperature, this, is how hot or cold the air is.

   **B** One thing it will tell you is the temperature. This is how hot or cold the air is.

   **C** One thing it will tell you is the temperature how hot or cold the air is.

   **D** As it is written.

**13** Which group of words is not a complete sentence? Write the number of the sentence.

   _____

   _____

   _____

   _____

**14** Which sentence best combines sentences 11 and 12 without changing their meaning?

   **F** It will tell you how hard the wind is blowing it will tell you from which direction it is coming.

   **G** It will tell you how hard the wind is blowing and from which direction it is coming.

   **H** How hard the wind is blowing and which direction it is from.

   **J** It will tell you which direction it is coming from it will tell you how hard the wind is blowing.

GO ON

**Answers**

**8** Ⓐ Ⓑ Ⓒ Ⓓ   **10** Ⓐ Ⓑ Ⓒ Ⓓ   **12** Ⓐ Ⓑ Ⓒ Ⓓ

**9** Ⓕ Ⓖ Ⓗ Ⓙ   **11** Ⓕ Ⓖ Ⓗ Ⓙ   **14** Ⓕ Ⓖ Ⓗ Ⓙ

Here is the next part of Loretta's rough draft for her report. This part has certain words and phrases underlined. Read the draft carefully. Then answer questions 15–22.

Storms are the violent and dangerous aspects of weather. The kind of
(14)                                                                                    (15)

storm we see <u>most often is the thunderstorm?</u> A thunderstorm happens
(16)

<u>when theres' a great</u> difference in the temperature between the air close

to the earth and the air higher up. A thunderstorm often happens on a
(17)

hot and muggy summer afternoon. The <u>hot air near the earth</u> is pushed
(18)

up by cooler air around it. Moisture-laden, threatening clouds form, and
(19)

it starts getting darker. Then lightning flashes, <u>thunder rolls and winds</u>
(20)

<u>blow</u>. The storm usually lasts a few minutes. <u>When it was over</u>, the sky
(21)                                                          (22)

usually clears.

Sometimes thunderstorms <u>come with Tornadoes</u>. A tornado is <u>the</u>
(23)                                                          (24)

<u>more violent kind of storm</u>. A tornado comes up suddenly. At first it looks
(25)                                                          (26)

like a thick dark cloud coming from a distance. Then <u>an funnel–shaped</u>
(27)

<u>piece</u> dangles down from the cloud. When the funnel touches the ground
(28)

it picks up everything in its path.

GO ON

**15** In sentence 15, <u>most often is the thunderstorm?</u> is best written—

A  most often is the thunderstorm.

B  more often is the thunderstorm?

C  most often is the thunderstorm!

D  As it is written.

**16** In sentence 16, <u>when theres' a great</u> is best written—

F  when theres a great

G  when ther'es a great

H  when there's a great

J  As it is written.

**17** In sentence 18, <u>hot air near the earth</u> is best written—

A  hot, air near the earth

B  hot air, near the earth

C  hot, air, near the earth

D  As it is written.

**18** In sentence 20, <u>thunder rolls and winds blow</u> is best written—

F  thunder rolls and winds, blow

G  thunder rolls, and winds blow

H  thunder, rolls and winds blow

J  As it is written.

**19** In sentence 22, <u>When it was over</u> is best written—

A  When it is over

B  When it has been over

C  When it will be over

D  As it is written.

**20** In sentence 23, <u>come with Tornadoes</u> is best written—

F  come with tornadoes

G  comes with tornadoes

H  comes with Tornadoes

J  As it is written.

**21** In sentence 24, <u>the more violent kind of storm</u> is best written—

A  the much more violent kind of storm

B  the more violenter kind of storm

C  the most violent kind of storm

D  As it is written.

**22** In sentence 27, <u>an funnel–shaped piece</u> is best written—

F  a funnel–shaped piece

G  an funnel–shaped piece,

H  an Funnel–Shaped piece

J  As it is written.

**Answers**

**15** Ⓐ Ⓑ Ⓒ Ⓓ    **17** Ⓐ Ⓑ Ⓒ Ⓓ    **19** Ⓐ Ⓑ Ⓒ Ⓓ    **21** Ⓐ Ⓑ Ⓒ Ⓓ
**16** Ⓕ Ⓖ Ⓗ Ⓙ    **18** Ⓕ Ⓖ Ⓗ Ⓙ    **20** Ⓕ Ⓖ Ⓗ Ⓙ    **22** Ⓕ Ⓖ Ⓗ Ⓙ

# Identifying Misspelled Words

Directions: Read each sentence carefully. If one of the words is misspelled, darken the circle for that word. If all the words are spelled correctly, then darken the circle for *No mistake*.

**TRY THIS**
Read each sentence carefully. If you are not sure of an answer, first decide which answer choices are spelled correctly. Then see if you can recognize the misspelled word from your reading experience.

**Sample A**

Hakim was <u>absint</u> from <u>class</u> on Tuesday. <u>No mistake</u>
       **A**      **B**    **C**     **D**

**THINK IT THROUGH**
The correct answer is <u>A</u>. All of the other words except <u>absint</u> are spelled correctly. <u>Absint</u> is spelled a-b-s-e-n-t.

---
🛑 STOP

1    Meryl was <u>dizzy</u> from <u>spinning</u> <u>around</u> so much. <u>No mistake</u>
          **A**         **B**   **C**        **D**

2    The <u>storm</u> produced <u>driveing</u> rain and <u>hail</u>. <u>No mistake</u>
       **F**           **G**       **H**  **J**

3    Birds <u>steak</u> out a <u>territory</u> when they are <u>nesting</u>. <u>No mistake</u>
         **A**      **B**           **C**     **D**

4    The <u>pair</u> that Beth bought was <u>ripe</u> and <u>sweet</u>. <u>No mistake</u>
       **F**             **G**   **H**   **J**

5    Mr. Chung <u>traveled</u> a <u>great</u> deal when he was <u>younger</u>. <u>No mistake</u>
           **A**    **B**          **C**    **D**

6    Lucia <u>received</u> an <u>imvitation</u> to the <u>birthday</u> party. <u>No mistake</u>
         **F**       **G**        **H**       **J**

7    There was a <u>livly</u> <u>debate</u> about expanding the park <u>system</u>. <u>No mistake</u>
           **A**  **B**              **C**    **D**

8    Roland <u>enjoys</u> eating <u>cereal</u> with <u>blueberrys</u> in it. <u>No mistake</u>
         **F**       **G**      **H**      **J**

---
🛑 STOP

**Answers**
SA Ⓐ Ⓑ Ⓒ Ⓓ    2 Ⓕ Ⓖ Ⓗ Ⓙ    4 Ⓕ Ⓖ Ⓗ Ⓙ    6 Ⓕ Ⓖ Ⓗ Ⓙ    8 Ⓕ Ⓖ Ⓗ Ⓙ
1 Ⓐ Ⓑ Ⓒ Ⓓ    3 Ⓐ Ⓑ Ⓒ Ⓓ    5 Ⓐ Ⓑ Ⓒ Ⓓ    7 Ⓐ Ⓑ Ⓒ Ⓓ

# Test

**Sample A**

**A Canadian Vacation**

Charley and his family spent a month vacationing in Canada. During that time they visited many places and had an exciting time. Charley wanted to tell his favorite aunt all about the places he visited, so he wrote her a letter.

Charley wants to locate some of the cities in Canada that he visited. He should look in—

A an index.

B an atlas.

C a newspaper.

D a table of contents.

Charley made a concept web to help him write his letter. Study the concept web and use it to answer questions 1 and 2.

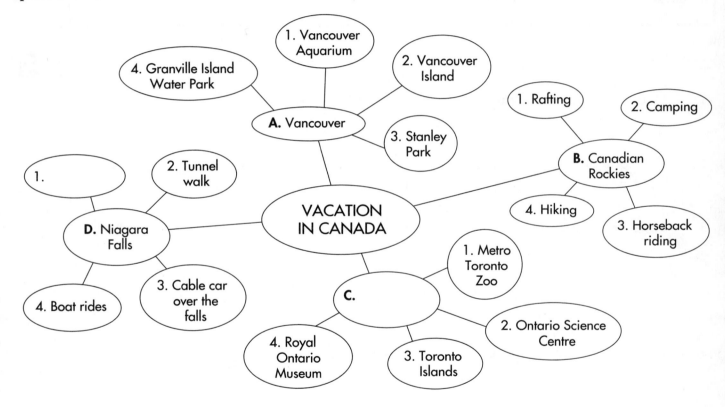

1  Which of these belongs in circle C?

A  Toronto

B  Montreal

C  Quebec City

D  Edmonton

2  Which of these belongs in number 1 around circle D?

F  Toronto library

G  Niagara Falls nature hikes

H  Montreal harbour cruises

J  Glacier National Park

**GO ON**

**Answers**
**SA** Ⓐ Ⓑ Ⓒ Ⓓ   **1** Ⓐ Ⓑ Ⓒ Ⓓ   **2** Ⓕ Ⓖ Ⓗ Ⓙ

**Here is a rough draft of the first part of Charley's letter. Read the rough draft carefully. Then answer questions 3–10.**

---

July 25

Dear Aunt Cynthia,

I want to tell you about the time we had in Canada that was
(1)

wonderful. We drove more than two thousand miles. We visited many
(2)                                                    (3)

places along the way. My friend went on vacation to Hawaii.
(4)

Niagara Falls was one of my favorite places I can't believe how
(5)

powerful that waterfall is! We took a boat ride. Right to the foot of the
(6)                    (7)

Falls. It's a good thing that we were wearing rain coats and rain hats!
(8)

We also took a cable car to view the Falls and viewed the Falls from
(9)

the top. That was quite a view! There is a beautiful park in Niagara
(10)                         (11)

Falls. We took a long nature hike through the park. We saw many
(12)                                        (13)

different kinds of plants along the hike.

We could see the Falls from the balcony of our hotel room. We went
(14)                                                    (15)

swimming every evening in the hotel pool.

---

GO ON

**3**  **What is the best way to write sentence 1?**

  **A**  I want to tell you about Canada and the wonderful time we had in Canada.

  **B**  I want to tell you about the wonderful time we had in Canada.

  **C**  The wonderful time we had in Canada I want to tell you about.

  **D**  As it is written.

**4**  **Which sentence best combines sentences 2 and 3 without changing their meaning?**

  **F**  More than two thousand miles, we drove, we visited many places along the way.

  **G**  Drove more than two thousand miles and visited many places along the way.

  **H**  We visited many places along the way and then drove more than two thousand miles.

  **J**  We drove more than two thousand miles and visited many places along the way.

**5**  **Which sentence does not belong in Charley's letter? Write the number.**

_____

_____

_____

_____

_____

**6**  **Which sentence needlessly repeats a word or a group of words?**

  **A**  2

  **B**  4

  **C**  8

  **D**  9

**7**  **The best way to write sentence 5 is—**

  **F**  Niagara Falls was one of my favorite places, I can't believe how powerful that waterfall is!

  **G**  Was one of my favorite places. I can't believe how powerful that waterfall is!

  **H**  Niagara Falls was one of my favorite places. I can't believe how powerful that waterfall is!

  **J**  As it is written.

**8**  **Which group of words is *not* a complete sentence?**

  **A**  3

  **B**  7

  **C**  11

  **D**  14

**9**  **What is the most colorful way to write sentence 13?**

  **F**  We saw numerous types of plants on our long hike.

  **G**  We saw a wide variety of interesting plants during our nature hike.

  **H**  We saw lots of different kinds of plants on our hike.

  **J**  As it is written.

**10**  **Which of the following sentences could be added after sentence 15?**

  **A**  There are many hotels in Niagara Falls.

  **B**  We sometimes swim in the pool in our park at home.

  **C**  I liked the hotel we stayed at in Niagara Falls.

  **D**  We could have also stayed at a motel.

**Answers**

**3** Ⓐ Ⓑ Ⓒ Ⓓ    **6** Ⓐ Ⓑ Ⓒ Ⓓ    **8** Ⓐ Ⓑ Ⓒ Ⓓ    **10** Ⓐ Ⓑ Ⓒ Ⓓ
**4** Ⓕ Ⓖ Ⓗ Ⓙ    **7** Ⓕ Ⓖ Ⓗ Ⓙ    **9** Ⓕ Ⓖ Ⓗ Ⓙ

**90**

Here is the next part of Charley's rough draft for his letter. This part has certain words and phrases underlined. Read the draft carefully. Then answer questions 11–18.

We had an exciting time in the canadian rockies. This part of
(16)                                                    (17)

Canada has tall mountains, huge waterfalls, and beautiful evergreen

trees. Driving through the mountains was so much fun.
      (18)

We did so many things in the mountains. One of the most exciting
(19)                                               (20)

was River Rafting. A professional rafter took us down the river. It was
      (21)                                                         (22)

funner than a roller coaster ride!

We spent several days camping in a national park. At night we saw
(23)                                               (24)

thousands of stars in the sky. It was fun to cook marshmallows over a
                                                           (25)

open fire. It was also fun to sleep in its tent. During the day we took long
      (26)                          (27)

hikes on the mountain trails. We saw many different animals on our hike?
            (28)

We also got a chance to go horseback riding. It was the first time that
(29)                   (30)

I was ever on a horse. The horse I rode was very gentle and easy to ride.
            (31)

Riding a horse was a great way to see the beautiful mountain scenery.
(32)

Your nephew.

Charley

GO ON

**11** In sentence 16, <u>in the canadian rockies</u> is best written—

**F** in the Canadian rockies

**G** in the Canadian Rockies

**H** in the canadian Rockies

**J** As it is written.

**12** In sentence 20, <u>was River Rafting</u> is best written—

**A** was River rafting

**B** was river Rafting

**C** was river rafting

**D** As it is written.

**13** In sentence 22, <u>was funner</u> is best written—

**F** was most fun

**G** was much funner

**H** was more fun

**J** As it is written.

**14** In sentence 25, <u>over a open fire</u> is best written—

**A** over an Open fire

**B** over a Open fire

**C** over an open fire

**D** As it is written.

**15** In sentence 26, <u>in its tent</u> is best written—

**F** in our tent

**G** in us tent

**H** in it's tent

**J** As it is written.

**16** In sentence 28, <u>on our hike?</u> is best written—

**A** on our hike!

**B** on our hike.

**C** on their hike?

**D** As it is written.

**17** In sentence 29, <u>to go horseback riding</u> is best written—

**F** to go horseback, riding

**G** to go, horseback riding

**H** to, go horseback riding

**J** As it is written.

**18** In the closing, <u>Your nephew.</u> is best written—

**A** Your nephew,

**B** Your nephew?

**C** Your nephew!

**D** As it is written.

GO ON

**Answers**

**11** Ⓕ Ⓖ Ⓗ Ⓙ  **13** Ⓕ Ⓖ Ⓗ Ⓙ  **15** Ⓕ Ⓖ Ⓗ Ⓙ  **17** Ⓕ Ⓖ Ⓗ Ⓙ

**12** Ⓐ Ⓑ Ⓒ Ⓓ  **14** Ⓐ Ⓑ Ⓒ Ⓓ  **16** Ⓐ Ⓑ Ⓒ Ⓓ  **18** Ⓐ Ⓑ Ⓒ Ⓓ

For questions 19–30, read each sentence carefully. If one of the words is misspelled, darken the circle for that word. If all the words are spelled correctly, then darken the circle for *No mistake.*

19    The dog kept whineing at the kitchen door. No mistake
           F      G                    H                    J

20    We were starttled by the loud explosion. No mistake
                    A              B        C              D

21    Thomas Edison was the imventor of the light bulb. No mistake
                                      F              G    H          J

22    He is a very popular guitar player. No mistake
                        A          B        C              D

23    The heat from the flames was very imtense. No mistake
           F                G                      H              J

24    Her abilitys are well above average. No mistake
              A                  B        C              D

25    The cat bolted for the aley when the dog barked. No mistake
                 F                G                      H          J

26    It is urgent that we return home immediately. No mistake
              A                  B                C              D

27    The plane flew threw the clouds. No mistake
              F          G        H              J

28    He recieved the missing package yesterday. No mistake
              A              B                C              D

29    Advertiseing can make your product known to the public. No mistake
           F                              G          H                        J

30    Gino has missed band practice latly. No mistake
                    A              B        C          D

**Answers**
19  (F) (G) (H) (J)    22  (A) (B) (C) (D)    25  (F) (G) (H) (J)    28  (A) (B) (C) (D)
20  (A) (B) (C) (D)    23  (F) (G) (H) (J)    26  (A) (B) (C) (D)    29  (F) (G) (H) (J)
21  (F) (G) (H) (J)    24  (A) (B) (C) (D)    27  (F) (G) (H) (J)    30  (A) (B) (C) (D)

93

## Reading Comprehension

**Sample A**

### Early Trains
The first trains in America were very different from modern trains. Horses pulled wagons on wooden rails. During the 1830s, the first steam engines were used. They burned wood for fuel.

**What did steam engines use for fuel?**

A  gas     C  wood

B  water     D  coal

For questions 1–46, carefully read each selection and the questions that follow. Then darken the circle for the correct answer, or write in the answer.

## Learning About King Cobras

King cobras are large, dangerous snakes that live in parts of Asia. These snakes often grow to be 18 feet long. This is the largest of all poisonous snakes in the world. The cobra has loose skin on either side of its neck. When the snake is angry or threatened, it spreads its long ribs and flattens its neck. The skin stands out and makes a *hood*.

King cobras mainly eat other snakes. The cobra has short fangs, but its poison is very strong. Many people have died from being bitten by these snakes.

The king cobra is the only snake that makes a nest. The mother finds a place with many leaves. She pushes the leaves together. Then she lays about 40 eggs. She covers them with more leaves. Then she lies on top of the nest for about two months until the young hatch. The father also stays nearby.

The babies can take care of themselves as soon as they are born. They are about 20 inches long. Even young cobras are very dangerous.

As dangerous as they are, cobras are famous as the partners of snake charmers. The hood creates quite an amazing appearance. During the snake charmer's act, the cobra appears to be affected by the music. Actually, as with all snakes, the cobra cannot hear. Instead, it responds to visual clues. Many snake charmers get a feeling of safety from the fact that cobras can have a rather slow strike.

You have 35 minutes to complete this test. Use the answer sheets in the back of the book to mark your answers.

**GO ON**

1   In what area of the world do king cobras live?

   A   Africa

   B   Asia

   C   Iceland

   D   North America

2   If you saw two king cobras lying on or near a pile of leaves, you might guess that—

   F   they are tired.

   G   they are hungry.

   H   they are enjoying the sun.

   J   they are protecting their eggs.

3   In this selection, what does *hood* mean?

   A   a hat

   B   poison spit by the cobra

   C   skin that stands out from the cobra's neck

   D   a nest

4   King cobras mainly eat—

   F   birds' eggs.

   G   leaves and berries.

   H   other snakes.

   J   small animals.

5   What does the nest of a king cobra look like?

   A   It is a big pile of leaves.

   B   It is made of branches.

   C   It is hidden high in a tree.

   D   It is made of rocks.

6   How long are adult king cobras?

_____

_____

_____

_____

_____

7   Which words from the selection show that a king cobra bite can be deadly?

   F   …poison is very strong.

   G   …spreads out its ribs…

   H   …responds to visual clues.

   J   …have a rather slow strike.

8   What is true of king cobras?

   A   Only the adult snakes are dangerous.

   B   They respond to snake charmers' music.

   C   They strike rapidly.

   D   They are the largest poisonous snakes in the world.

9   To find out more about king cobras, you should—

   F   travel to Asia.

   G   read a reference book about snakes.

   H   read a travel book about Asia.

   J   look for snakes in your neighborhood.

10   What is this selection mainly about?

   A   what king cobras eat

   B   where king cobras live

   C   what king cobras are like

   D   a kind of dangerous snake

▶GO ON▶

# The Talking Banana

It was May, and Chris was ready for summer vacation to begin. He didn't want to get up at 6:00 A.M. to catch the bus. He didn't want to do his math homework. And most of all, he didn't want to write. Every Monday, Wednesday, and Friday his class wrote in their journals. Chris had written about a thousand things—spring break, his sister, his bike, even his pet German shepherd, Rusty. He couldn't think of one more thing to write about!

His teacher, Ms. Crain, said there were lots of things to write about. She said, "Write about what you had for breakfast this morning." So Chris wrote, "I had cereal for breakfast." He sat for a long time trying to think of something else to say. Finally, he added, "I put a banana on top of the cereal."

The next time Ms. Crain walked around the room, she read the two sentences. "Oh dear," she said. "I can tell that you need some inspiration. I think I have just what you need." She went back to her desk and pulled out a rectangular box. She opened it and handed Chris a sleek gold pen. Then she whispered, "This is a special pen. It will help you get some ideas."

Chris looked at the pen doubtfully. Slowly, he put it near the paper. The pen wrote, "The banana was from Brazil. It began talking to me." Chris couldn't believe it. He waited for the pen to write more, but it didn't.

Chris wrote that the banana said its name was Joey and that Chris wouldn't believe what had happened to it! Chris and the pen took turns writing the story. For the first time ever, he was sorry when Ms. Crain said writing time was over. Chris read his story aloud the next day. He called it "The Life of a Banana." It read as follows:

## The Life of a Banana

Yesterday I had cereal for breakfast. I put a banana on top of the cereal. The banana was from Brazil. It began talking to me. The banana said that its name was Joey and that I wouldn't believe what had happened to it!

Joey told me about being raised on a plantation with millions of other bananas. Joey was as happy as could be, growing in a clump with ten or fifteen other bananas. Joey liked lying in the tropical sun and daydreaming about banana cream pie, banana splits, and other fabulous banana desserts.

All of this came to an end a week ago. A plantation worker suddenly appeared carrying a big knife. He whacked Joey's clump off the banana plant and left it on the ground. Later, another worker picked up the clump and put it with other clumps in a big wooden *crate*. The crate was put onto a truck and taken to a seaport. Joey and hundreds of other bananas were loaded onto a ship that sailed to the United States. Soon my mom was buying Joey and his friends in the supermarket.

Joey said he felt better after we talked. But I still think he was a little disappointed that he didn't end up in a banana cream pie or something more exciting than cereal.

GO ON

**11** According to the selection, when does Chris write his story?

F   in July

G   in November

H   in April

J   in May

**12** Why didn't Chris want to write in his journal?

_____

_____

_____

_____

_____

_____

**13** What did Ms. Crain give to Chris to help him write?

A   a banana

B   a special pen

C   a rectangular box

D   a good grade

**14** Why was Chris sorry when Ms. Crain said that writing time was over?

F   He wanted to make a good grade.

G   He did not want to go to science class.

H   He wanted to keep writing.

J   He did not have his math homework finished.

**15** In this story, the word *crate* means—

A   supermarket.

B   ship.

C   box.

D   truck.

**16** In order to answer number 15, the reader should—

F   reread the first line of each paragraph.

G   reread the last paragraph of the story.

H   look for the word *crate* in the story.

J   reread the title of the story.

**17** Where was the banana from?

A   a farm in the Midwest

B   a forest in California

C   a ranch in Central America

D   a plantation in Brazil

**18** How do you think Chris will feel when it's time to write in the journal again?

F   bored

G   angry

H   eager

J   sad

**19** How can you tell this story was a fantasy?

A   Students wrote in their journals.

B   A banana talked.

C   Bananas were grown on a plantation.

D   A teacher gave a student a pen.

**20** If this story continued, what would probably happen next?

F   Someone else would write an interesting story with Ms. Crain's special pen.

G   Chris would talk to a carrot.

H   Chris would do his math homework.

J   Chris' dad would make a banana cream pie.

GO ON

# Making a Clay Pot

**Choose a simple item to create from clay. It might be a pot, bowl, cup, or flower vase. Follow these directions:**

1. Take a piece of clay about the size of an apple. Press and squeeze it on a flat surface until there are no lumps or air bubbles.
2. Use both hands to shape the clay into a smooth, round ball.
3. Put the ball of clay in your left hand. With the thumb of your right hand, make an opening in the clay. Press down toward your palm, leaving a half inch of clay at the bottom to make the floor of your pot.
4. Press the clay gently between your thumb and fingers. Turn the pot after each squeeze to make it thin out evenly. Continue until it is as thin as you want it.
5. Cover the pot with plastic so it doesn't dry too quickly and allow it to dry for several days. Take off the plastic and wait several more days.
6. When the pot is completely dry, it is ready to be *fired* in a special oven called a *kiln*. After firing, the pot will keep its shape.

GO ON

**21** The first thing you should do when making a clay pot is—

A press and squeeze the clay.

B cover the clay in plastic.

C shape the clay into a ball.

D make the floor of the pot.

**22** What is something you should *not* do when making a clay pot?

F remove the lumps from the clay

G squeeze the clay between your thumb and fingers

H shape the clay into a smooth, round ball

J let the pot dry quickly

**23** The selection tells about making a clay pot by doing all of the following *except*—

A letting the pot dry.

B firing the pot.

C pressing the clay.

D painting or carving designs.

**24** A pot that has been *fired* has been—

F broken.

G covered.

H baked.

J melted.

**25** Why should the pot be turned after each squeeze?

_____

_____

_____

_____

_____

**26** According to the directions, which of the following is *not* needed to make a pot?

A plastic

B a kiln

C paint

D clay

**27** Firing is important because it—

F thins out the pot.

G makes the pot smaller.

H allows the pot to keep its shape.

J adds designs to the pot.

**28** You can tell that a kiln is a kind of—

A flat surface.

B clay mixture.

C bowl.

D oven.

**29** This selection would probably appear in a book called—

F *Easy Arts and Crafts.*

G *How to Build a Kiln.*

H *The History of Ancient Arts.*

J *The Mystery of Clay Mountain.*

▶GO ON▶

# A Wonderful Woman

"Mama, look over there. Isn't that Jane Addams?" asked Erich.

"Yes, yes, you are correct. That is Jane Addams. I would know her anywhere. She helped me settle into the American way of life when I first moved here from Germany," replied Mrs. Schroeder.

"What do you mean, Mama?" asked Erich.

"When I first came to Chicago in 1890, I could not speak any English. I did not have a job. I am afraid that I did not know anyone either. I was only 19 years old and I was determined to become an American citizen and a successful person in the United States, but it was difficult. I heard about Jane Addams' Hull House from another German immigrant. She told me that I could go to Hull House and learn English and become accustomed to life in the United States," answered Mrs. Schroeder.

"Did you go to Hull House, Mama?" asked Erich.

"I went there as soon as I could. I signed up for an evening class to learn English. The social workers at Hull House were able to get me a job, too. It was not a great job—I stocked shelves at a small local grocery store, but it was a living. The social workers also helped me find a safe place to live. I shared a room in an apartment with two other women about my age. It worked out fine," said Mrs. Schroeder.

"Did you ever talk to Jane Addams?" queried Erich.

"Jane Addams made a point to talk to all the people who came to Hull House. After I finished my English classes, she asked to meet with me. She told me how I could become an American citizen. I took more classes at Hull House. This time I learned about the government of the United States. It was in this class that I met your father. He and I became American citizens in the same naturalization ceremony," explained Mrs. Schroeder.

"Why did Jane Addams help establish Hull House?" wondered Erich. "She knew how to speak English."

"She was a humanitarian. She saw a need for a community center that would help immigrants, young and old alike, keep from becoming *impoverished* and help them become upstanding American citizens. She is my hero," stated Mrs. Schroeder.

GO ON

**30** According to the selection, why did Mrs. Schroeder come to the United States?

A She wanted to search for gold.

B She hoped to learn to speak English.

C She wanted to find a job in a grocery store.

D She wanted to become a citizen of the United States.

**31** How did Mrs. Schroeder find out about Hull House?

F Another German immigrant told her.

G She heard about it while she was still in Germany.

H She read a newspaper article about Hull House.

J Jane Addams invited her to come to Hull House.

**32** What did Mrs. Schroeder have to do to become a citizen of the United States?

_____

_____

_____

_____

_____

_____

_____

_____

**33** Which word best describes Jane Addams?

A pitiless

B rash

C wealthy

D compassionate

**34** In this selection, the word *impoverished* means—

F affluent.

G impossible.

H poor.

J sent back to the native country.

**35** According to the story, Hull House helped immigrants in all of the following ways *except*—

A finding jobs.

B finding safe places to live.

C finding a way back to their native country.

D learning to speak English.

**36** From the story, you can tell that Mrs. Schroeder is—

F easily frightened.

G brave and determined.

H disappointed in the United States.

J angry with Jane Addams.

**37** What would be another good title for this story?

A "The Life of Erich Schroeder"

B "Learning at Hull House"

C "The History of Chicago"

D "Immigrant Life"

GO ON

# Visiting Pioneer City

Welcome to Pioneer City! Here you can learn about how the pioneers of the 1800s lived. These buildings are preserved through the efforts of local conservationists. We keep history alive!

The tour begins at the old schoolhouse. Take a look at the slates and inkwells used by the children. Notice that this schoolhouse had two fireplaces to help keep young learners warm!

When you walk out the schoolhouse door, turn right and walk about the length of a city block. You'll come to the storefronts. The first two are closed, but you are invited to go into the General Store. Find out what families stocked up on and what the bargains were back then.

Go directly across the street from the General Store to Minnie's Well. A large group of community members dug the well together.

From the well, go back north toward the schoolhouse. You can peek into the bank, but there is no longer any money there!

Directly behind the bank is the Rose Hotel. You can go as far as the fancy front desk, but the upstairs is closed. Be sure to flip through the guest registry—one of your relatives might have stayed there.

From the hotel, go back north to the schoolhouse and out to the parking lot. We hope you enjoyed your visit!

GO ON

**38** This poster was written in order to—

    **F** describe pioneer life.

    **G** congratulate local conservationists.

    **H** give directions for the tour.

    **J** raise money for the community.

**39** About how far is it from the schoolhouse to the stores?

    **A** the length of a city block

    **B** two miles

    **C** two steps

    **D** the length of three city blocks

**40** To get from the well to the bank, you should—

    **F** go across the street.

    **G** go north toward the schoolhouse.

    **H** turn right and walk about a city block.

    **J** walk directly behind the well.

**41** What is directly behind the bank?

_____

_____

_____

_____

_____

_____

**42** Which of these is not permitted at the Rose Hotel?

    **A** going upstairs

    **B** flipping through the guest registry

    **C** looking at the front desk

    **D** closing the door

**43** What two attractions will you see between the well and returning to the schoolhouse?

    **F** the bank and the Rose Hotel

    **G** the bank and the General Store

    **H** the Rose Hotel and the General Store

    **J** the library and the hat shop

**44** According to the poster, you can see all of the following at Pioneer City *except*—

    **A** a bank.

    **B** a schoolhouse.

    **C** a blacksmith shop.

    **D** a well.

**45** You can tell that the tour is meant to be—

    **F** led by a tour guide.

    **G** provided only for historians.

    **H** a complete picture of pioneer life.

    **J** self-guided.

**46** From the poster, you can tell that local conservationists think it is important to—

    **A** make good grades.

    **B** play sports.

    **C** keep history alive.

    **D** follow directions.

**STOP**

## Reading Vocabulary

**Sample A**

**Terrified means—**

A delighted    C frightened

B completed    D puzzled

For questions 1–9, darken the circle for the word or words that have the same or almost the same meaning as the underlined word.

**1**   To **permit** is to—

A allow

B teach

C measure

D realize

**2**   To **quit** means the same as to—

F begin

G stop

H continue

J start

**3**   **Miserable** means—

A joyful

B scared

C unhappy

D confused

**4**   **Cruel** means the same as—

F little

G mean

H protected

J strange

**5**   If something is **fragile**, it is—

A very dry

B easily broken

C shiny

D colorful

**6**   **Frequently** means—

F never

G always

H often

J yearly

**7**   A **wail** is a kind of—

A cry

B shoe

C tool

D store

**8**   A **scheme** is a kind of—

F party

G song

H report

J plan

**9**   **Brisk** means the same as—

A silly

B quick

C difficult

D lonely

**GO ON**

 You have 20 minutes to complete this test. Use the answer sheets in the back of the book to mark your answers.

**104**

**Sample B**

> People are often remembered for their <u>conduct</u>.

In which sentence does <u>conduct</u> have the same meaning as it does in the sentence above?

A  I try to <u>conduct</u> myself with the best manners possible.

B  What are some objects that can <u>conduct</u> electricity?

C  Mr. Green will <u>conduct</u> the orchestra this evening.

D  Leticia is proud of her school <u>conduct</u>.

For questions 10–14, darken the circle for the sentence in which the underlined word means the same as it does in the sentence in the box.

**10**

> If we can agree on payment, then we have a <u>deal</u>.

In which sentence does <u>deal</u> have the same meaning as it does in the sentence above?

F  Kara and Jeff made a <u>deal</u> to trade baseball cards.

G  I will <u>deal</u> with them later.

H  Is it my turn to <u>deal</u> the cards?

J  There is a good <u>deal</u> of work left to be done.

**11**

> We sat under the <u>shade</u> of a big oak tree.

In which sentence does <u>shade</u> have the same meaning as it does in the sentence above?

A  Please pull down the window <u>shade</u>.

B  Ramon will use his pencil to <u>shade</u> his map.

C  The awning created a spot of <u>shade</u>.

D  This is the most beautiful <u>shade</u> of purple.

**12**

> The judges will <u>grade</u> our performance.

In which sentence does <u>grade</u> have the same meaning as it does in the sentence above?

F  My brother is in the seventh <u>grade</u> at St. Paul School.

G  Ms. Henning will <u>grade</u> our math tests.

H  The truck slowly went up the steep <u>grade</u>.

J  We usually try to buy the best <u>grade</u> of eggs.

**13**

> My cousin is staying in our <u>spare</u> room.

In which sentence does <u>spare</u> have the same meaning as it does in the sentence above?

A  The knight decided to <u>spare</u> the dragon.

B  We cannot <u>spare</u> the money for the trip.

C  I will <u>spare</u> you the time and expense of doing it yourself.

D  Please check my <u>spare</u> tire.

**14**

> The Spanish club will <u>meet</u> for two hours.

In which sentence does <u>meet</u> have the same meaning as it does in the sentence above?

F  Our class will <u>meet</u> in the gym.

G  Sandra will run in the track <u>meet</u>.

H  The newspaper reporter had a deadline to <u>meet</u>.

J  I'd like you to <u>meet</u> my grandfather.

▶GO ON▶

**Sample C**

Because it has small parts, that toy is not <u>suitable</u> for a young child. <u>Suitable</u> means—

A   neat

B   acceptable

C   funny

D   serious

For questions 15–22, darken the circle for the word or words that give the meaning of the underlined word.

15   Our <u>compact</u> camping gear easily fits into the van. <u>Compact</u> means—

A   large

B   stiff

C   compressed

D   loose

16   They lived in a <u>remote</u> cabin far back in the woods. <u>Remote</u> means—

F   army

G   concrete

H   manufactured

J   distant

17   Most people have to learn how to get along with both friends and <u>foes</u>. <u>Foes</u> means—

A   tricks

B   enemies

C   companions

D   families

18   Parent volunteers will <u>transport</u> the team and all its equipment to the game. <u>Transport</u> means—

F   move

G   make

H   send

J   receive

19   The clerk was very <u>courteous</u> and helpful. <u>Courteous</u> means—

A   stiff

B   polite

C   sleepy

D   fast

20   The hospital has a <u>mobile</u> clinic that comes to schools often. <u>Mobile</u> means—

F   special

G   safe

H   modern

J   movable

21   Both work and <u>leisure</u> are important. <u>Leisure</u> means—

A   sleep

B   free time

C   fast food

D   friendly

22   Molly said that helping us out wasn't a <u>burden</u>. <u>Burden</u> means—

F   gift

G   job

H   hardship

J   pleasure

## Part 1: Math Problem Solving

**Sample A**

What number makes the number sentence true?

$$3 + (2 + \square) = (3 + 2) + 7$$

A  2

B  3

C  5

D  7

— STOP

For questions 1–49, darken the circle for the correct answer, or write in the answer.

**1** Which expression will correctly complete the number sentence $4 + 6 = \square$?

A  $6 + 4$         C  $6 \times 4$

B  $10 - 4$        D  $10 + 4$

**2** Mrs. Wilson's students have art class on odd-numbered days during the school week. Use the calendar below to find how many days the students have art class this month.

| S | M | T | W | T | F | S |
|---|---|---|---|---|---|---|
|   |   | 1 | 2 | 3 | 4 | 5 |
| 6 | 7 | 8 | 9 | 10 | 11 | 12 |
| 13 | 14 | 15 | 16 | 17 | 18 | 19 |
| 20 | 21 | 22 | 23 | 24 | 25 | 26 |
| 27 | 28 | 29 | 30 |   |   |   |

F  10         H  15

G  11         J  30

**3**

| Famous Rivers | |
|---|---|
| **Name** | **Length (in miles)** |
| Amazon | 4,000 |
| Congo | 2,900 |
| Huang He | 2,903 |
| Mekong | 2,600 |
| Nile | 4,145 |
| Volga | 2,194 |
| Yangtze | 3,915 |

Which river is longer than the Congo but shorter than the Yangtze?

A  Huang He         C  Volga

B  Nile              D  Mekong

**4** Which number has an eight in the thousands place and a two in the hundreds place?

F  2,845         H  8,024

G  6,821         J  8,239

**5** What number would be placed third if these numbers were arranged in order from least to greatest?

| 5,291 | 5,921 | 4,073 | 4,628 | 5,601 |
|---|---|---|---|---|

A  5,601         C  5,291

B  4,628         D  5,921

**6** What number is expressed by this number sentence?

$$(4 \times 1,000) + (9 \times 100) + (2 \times 1)$$

F  4,920         H  4,092

G  4,902         J  492

**GO ON**

You have 50 minutes to complete this test. Use the answer sheets in the back of the book to mark your answers.

**7** Julie, Jay, Juan, and Cynthia had fun making patterns with their names. They counted the letters in their first names and arranged their names in order from the shortest to the longest name. Which list shows this arrangement?

A Julie, Juan, Jay, Cynthia

B Juan, Julie, Cynthia, Jay

C Cynthia, Julie, Jay, Juan

D Jay, Juan, Julie, Cynthia

**8** Write the numeral 2,605 in words.

_____

_____

_____

_____

**9** What number makes the number sentence true?

$$1 \times \square = 7$$

_____

_____

_____

_____

**10** Julia buys fabric to make pillows. Which list shows the amounts of fabric Julia buys in order from the least amount to the greatest amount?

| Fabric | Amount |
|---|---|
| Yellow calico | $\frac{1}{2}$ yard |
| Blue chambray | $\frac{2}{3}$ yard |
| Green cotton | $\frac{1}{5}$ yard |
| White muslin | $\frac{1}{4}$ yard |

F  $\frac{1}{5}, \frac{1}{4}, \frac{1}{2}, \frac{2}{3}$     H  $\frac{1}{2}, \frac{1}{5}, \frac{2}{3}, \frac{1}{4}$

G  $\frac{1}{4}, \frac{2}{3}, \frac{1}{2}, \frac{1}{5}$     J  $\frac{1}{2}, \frac{1}{4}, \frac{2}{3}, \frac{1}{5}$

**11** Which decimal shows the part of the figure that is shaded?

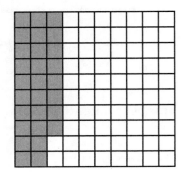

A  0.78          C  0.28

B  0.72          D  0.22

**12** Which figure shows $\frac{3}{5}$ shaded?

F          H

G          J

**13** Which mixed number tells what part of the figures are shaded?

A  $1\frac{3}{4}$          C  $1\frac{2}{7}$

B  $1\frac{1}{2}$          D  $1\frac{5}{7}$

**14** Which number sentence is in the same fact family as 10 − 2 = 8?

F  10 + 2 = 12     H  8 + 2 = 10

G  10 ÷ 2 = 5      J  8 − 2 = 6

GO ON

**15** Which two numbers can be written in the number sentence to make it correct?

$$(2 + 4) + \square = (3 + \square) + 5$$

A  6 and 3

B  7 and 4

C  3 and 2

D  6 and 4

**16** Yoshi buys some clothes. The table below shows how much she spends on each item.

| Clothing | Amount |
|----------|--------|
| Shirt | $21.95 |
| Shorts | $12.50 |
| Shoes | $19.72 |
| Swimsuit | $15.25 |

Which item has a price with a two in the tenths place?

F  Shirt

G  Shorts

H  Shoes

J  Swimsuit

This chart shows the number of people who want to take classes at the recreation center.

| Class | Number of People |
|-------|------------------|
| Art | ⅢⅡ ⅢⅡ |
| Dance | ⅢⅡ IIII |
| Swimming | III |
| Tennis | ⅢⅡ I |

**17** How many people want to take swimming and tennis classes?

A  3

B  6

C  9

D  10

The table below shows the names and times of some local radio programs. Study the table. Use it to answer questions 18–20.

|  | 9:00-9:30 | 9:30-10:00 | 10:00-10:30 | 10:30-11:00 |
|--|-----------|------------|-------------|-------------|
| **Station KBJB** | Sports | Update News | Green Thumb Hour | |
| **Station KHFB** | Golden Oldie Music | | Jazz Music | Jazz Music |

**18** Which program begins at 10:00 and ends at 11:00?

_____

_____

_____

_____

_____

_____

**19** Which program begins at 9:00 and ends at 10:00 on station KHFB?

F  "Jazz Music"

G  "Green Thumb Hour"

H  "Update News"

J  "Golden Oldie Music"

**20** What time does the program "Sports" end?

A  9:00

B  9:30

C  10:00

D  10:30

▶GO ON▶

The graph shows how many inches of rain fell in one year in Westwood. Study the graph. Use it to answer questions 21–23.

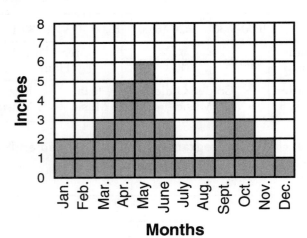

**Months**

**21** How many more inches did it rain in September than in July?

_____

_____

_____

_____

_____

_____

**22** How many inches did it rain altogether in April and November?

**F** 2 inches

**G** 3 inches

**H** 5 inches

**J** 7 inches

**23** Which month had 4 inches of rain?

**A** February

**B** May

**C** September

**D** November

**24** What shape does this picture have?

**F** diamond

**G** rectangle

**H** square

**J** oval

**25** If Manuel spins the spinner many times, which month will the spinner point to most often?

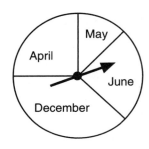

**A** December

**B** June

**C** May

**D** April

**26** Ted puts these cards in a box. If he reaches into the box and picks one card without looking, which card will it most likely be?

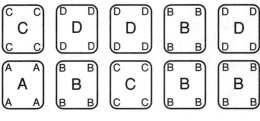

**F** A                 **H** C

**G** B                 **J** D

GO ON

**27**

I have 4 sides that are exactly the same. What am I?

Which figure shown here answers the riddle?

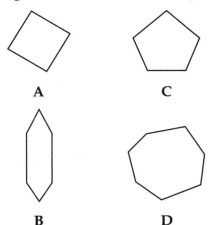

A           C

B           D

**28**   Liza drew this figure on her paper.

1

What did it look like when she turned it upside down?

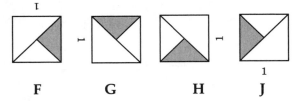

F      G      H      J

**29**   The graph shows the location of some shapes. What shape is located at (D, 4)?

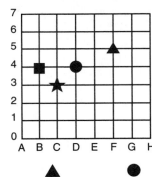

★      ▲      ●      ■

A      B      C      D

**30**   Look at the angles labeled on the figure shown here.

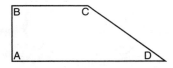

Which of these angles matches angle A?

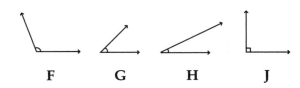

F      G      H      J

**31**   Which figure can be folded on the dotted line so that the two sides match exactly?

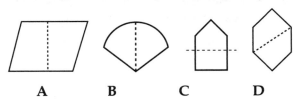

A      B      C      D

**32**   Trudy has these bills. She buys this toy bear.

How much money will Trudy have left?

_____

_____

_____

_____

_____

_____

GO ON

**33** What temperature does the picture most likely show?

**F** 18°F

**G** 39°F

**H** 51°F

**J** 92°F

**34** Which unit of measurement is best to describe the height of a building?

**A** inches

**B** feet

**C** pounds

**D** miles

**35** Which figure shows the least area of square units shaded?

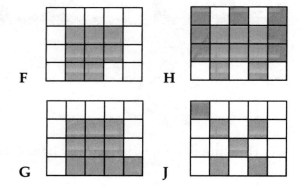

**36** Which nail is the shortest?

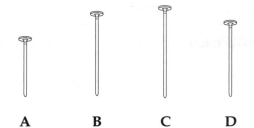

A    B    C    D

**37** Samantha has these coins.

Which group of coins shows the same value?

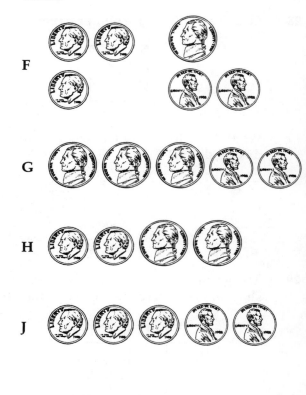

**▶ GO ON**

**38** Julissa played the piano for 35 minutes. She started playing at 3:15. Which of these clocks shows the time that Julissa stopped playing the piano?

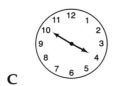
A

C

B

D

**39** Which unit of measurement is best to measure a window?

F   inches

G   yards

H   cups

J   miles

**40** The first thermometer shows the temperature before Tricia played a baseball game. The second thermometer shows the temperature when the game was over.

Before Game

95° ─┤    ├─ °F

90° ─┤

85° ─┤

After Game

95° ─┤    ├─ °F

90° ─┤

85° ─┤

What is the difference in the temperature after the game than before the game?

A   5° warmer

B   5° cooler

C   10° warmer

D   10° cooler

**41** Use your centimeter ruler. How long is the rocket ship from end to end?

F   2 centimeters

G   3 centimeters

H   4 centimeters

J   5 centimeters

**42** Use your inch ruler to help you answer this question.

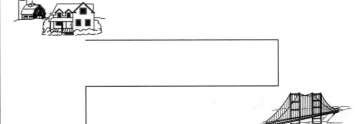

On this map, what is the length of the path from the farm to the bridge?

_____

_____

_____

_____

**43** There are 3 tennis balls in a can. Pat needs 27 tennis balls for tennis camp. Which number sentence shows how to find the number of cans he will need to buy?

A   27 + 3 = ☐        C   27 − 13 = ☐

B   27 × 3 = ☐        D   27 ÷ 3 = ☐

▶GO ON▶

**44**  A theater seats 285 people. The play now showing has 9 sold-out performances. Estimate how many people all together will see the play.

F   30        H   3,000

G   300      J   30,000

**45**  How many stars are inside the square and outside the circle?

_____

_____

_____

_____

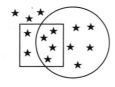

**46**  Which two shapes come next in the pattern?

A

B  (black triangle)(white triangle)

C  (white triangle)(white square)

D  (white square)(white triangle)

**47**  Marco took a box of popsicles to the park. He ate one and gave one to each of 5 friends. What do you need to know to find out how many popsicles Marco has left?

F   how many friends chose grape popsicles

G   how many popsicles were in the box

H   how many boxes of popsicles Marco ate at home

J   how many orange popsicles were in the box

**48**  Mrs. Sanchez owns a furniture store in Blue Mound. She needs to deliver a chair to a customer in Bruster. She uses the map to find the shortest distance between Blue Mound and Bruster. Estimate *about* how far Mrs. Sanchez will drive one way.

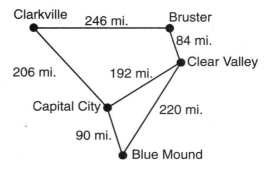

A   500 miles      C   300 miles

B   400 miles      D   200 miles

The shuttle bus at the airport departs from the terminal to the parking garage according to the following schedule.

| Shuttle Schedule |
| --- |
| 9:06 A.M. |
| 9:12 A.M. |
| 9:18 A.M. |
| 9:24 A.M. |
| 9:30 A.M. |

**49**  If the shuttle bus continues this pattern, at what time will the first shuttle depart the terminal after 11:15 A.M.?

F   11:00 A.M.

G   11:06 A.M.

H   11:12 A.M.

J   11:18 A.M.

STOP

# Part 2: Math Procedures

**Sample A**

$$7)\overline{87}$$

A 11
B 10 R1
C 12
D 12 R3
E NH

**STOP**

For questions 1–15, darken the circle for the correct answer. Darken the circle for *NH, Not Here,* if the correct answer is not given. If no choices are given, write in the answer.

**1**

$$\begin{array}{r} 59 \\ \times\ 33 \\ \hline \end{array}$$

A 334
B 1,947
C 3,340
D 19,470
E NH

**2**

$$\begin{array}{r} 721 \\ \times\ 4 \\ \hline \end{array}$$

F 2,884
G 2,864
H 2,184
J 2,164
K NH

**3**

$$5)\overline{75}$$

A 10
B 12
C 15
D 18
E NH

**4**

$$\begin{array}{r} 300 \\ -\ 62 \\ \hline \end{array}$$

F 362
G 348
H 248
J 238
K NH

**5**

$$927 + 32 + 649 = \square$$

A 1,598
B 1,608
C 1,680
D 1,806
E NH

**6**

$$3)\overline{939}$$

F 323
G 313
H 331
J 13
K NH

**7**

$$8 \times 6 = \square$$

A 2
B 14
C 42
D 48
E NH

**8**

$$24 \div 6 = \square$$

_____
_____
_____
_____
_____

**9** At work, Al put 129 cans of soup from one box on a shelf. The box held 235 cans. How many cans were left in the box?

F 102
G 106
H 116
J 114
K NH

**GO ON**

You have 15 minutes to complete this test. Use the answer sheets in the back of the book to mark your answers.

115

**Sample B**

Sharon has 12 carrots. She wants to share them equally with 3 horses.

How many carrots will each horse get?

A  36

B  15

C  5

D  4

E  NH

**STOP**

---

**10**  There are 11 cats on Josephine's farm. Each cat has 4 kittens. How many kittens are there altogether on the farm?

A  7

B  15

C  44

D  54

E  NH

**11**  Mr. Richards drove 2,531 miles while on vacation. *About* how many miles is that rounded to the nearest hundred?

F  2,500

G  2,530

H  2,600

J  3,000

K  NH

**12**  There are 16 sailboats that will race across the lake. They will sail in groups of 5.

How many extra boats are there?

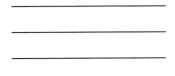

---

**13**  Mrs. Wong is going to paint the living room. She wants to buy these paint supplies.

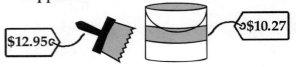

How much will the brush and paint cost before tax?

A  $22.22

B  $22.53

C  $23.22

D  $32.53

E  NH

**14**  The students in Ms. Jackson's class took a poll to see which fruit most children liked. Out of 32 students, 15 liked apples the most and 9 liked bananas the most. The rest liked oranges.

How many students liked oranges?

F  6

G  8

H  24

J  27

K  NH

**15**  Fran made 36 bibs to sell at a craft fair. She made 19 bibs from blue fabric and the rest of the bibs from pink fabric. How many bibs were made from pink fabric?

A  16

B  27

C  45

D  55

E  NH

**STOP**

## Listening

**Sample A**

    **A** liquid     **C** hard

    **B** solid     **D** sticky

**For questions 1–13, darken the circle for the word or words that best complete the sentence you hear.**

**1**  **A** sudden    **C** accidental

    **B** gradual    **D** tearful

**2**  **F** make a map of

    **G** march toward

    **H** escape to

    **J** settle along

**3**  **A** confused    **C** rich

    **B** eager    **D** lazy

**4**  **F** announce    **H** shrink

    **G** swing    **J** break off

**5**  **A** give advice

    **B** find a mistake

    **C** offer to help

    **D** praise too much

**6**  **F** soft

    **G** sad

    **H** skillful

    **J** surprising

**7**  **A** lying    **C** daring

    **B** careful    **D** bored

**8**  **F** normal

    **G** ordinary

    **H** grateful

    **J** strange

**9**  **A** praise

    **B** laugh aloud

    **C** find fault

    **D** leave

**10**  **F** send

    **G** shower

    **H** estimate

    **J** model

**11**  **A** silly

    **B** mean

    **C** loyal

    **D** sneaky

**12**  **F** be without

    **G** build up

    **H** gain

    **J** use

**13**  **A** loud noise

    **B** thought

    **C** calmness

    **D** serious problem

 You have 25 minutes to complete this test. Use the answer sheets in the back of the book to mark your answers.

**Sample B**

    **A** to read

    **B** to go to the beach

    **C** to study famous people

    **D** to go to school

STOP

**For questions 14–25, listen to the story. Then darken the circle for the word or words that best answer the question.**

**14**   **F** library     **H** store

     **G** mall       **J** park

**15**   **A** a dog

     **B** a princess

     **C** a puppet

     **D** a wizard

**16**   **F** a conversation

     **G** a newspaper article

     **H** a letter

     **J** a story

**17**   **A** movies

     **B** bumper cars

     **C** boat rides

     **D** miniature golf

**18**   **F** mention the ad

     **G** bring a group of four or more

     **H** bring a coupon

     **J** ask the manager

**19**   **A** make gingerbread

     **B** make a frozen banana treat

     **C** make cookies

     **D** make an ice cream sundae

**20**   **F** peel the banana

     **G** put the banana in the freezer

     **H** dip the banana in honey again

     **J** roll the banana in coconut

**21**   **A** list the various activities offered at the community center

     **B** give instructions to the center volunteers

     **C** advertise the events held at the community center

     **D** list the teachers and classes offered at the community center

**22**   **F** garden show

     **G** gymnastics competition

     **H** fall banquet

     **J** spring fiesta

**23**   **A** Mr. Weiss

     **B** Ms. Dole

     **C** Mr. Yasuda

     **D** Mrs. Allen

**24**   **F** a gardening class

     **G** a pottery class

     **H** a cake decorating class

     **J** an exercise class

**25**   **A** decorating the gym

     **B** planting a vegetable garden

     **C** the community center's director

     **D** the pottery teacher

STOP

## Language

Joan's class is learning about different regions of the world. They are learning about forest regions, grassland regions, and desert regions. The students are to locate the regions and determine the kinds of plants and animals that are found there. Joan decided to do a report about deserts. She found information about deserts that surprised her.

**Sample A**

Joan wants to locate the deserts in North and South America. She should look in—

A   an encyclopedia.

B   an atlas.

C   a newspaper.

D   an index.

**STOP**

For questions 1–26, darken the circle for the correct answer, or write in the answer.

1   Joan heard that a city in a desert in the United States is concerned about having enough water for people to use. Where could she find more information about this?

A   an atlas

B   a dictionary

C   a history book

D   the *Readers' Guide to Periodical Literature*

2   Which guide words might mark the page on which Joan would find the word *arid*?

F   arm–arose

G   argue–arithmetic

H   around–arrow

J   artery–article

3   Which of these should *not* be included in Joan's report?

A   the definition of a desert

B   where deserts are found

C   the kinds of animals found in a desert

D   where forest regions are found

4   Joan found a book called *Living Things of the Desert*. Where should she look to find a chapter about reptiles in the desert?

F   the table of contents

G   the title page

H   the glossary

J   the index

5   Joan wanted to look up the meaning of some words. She should look in—

A   an atlas.        C   a table of contents.

B   an encyclopedia.  D   a dictionary.

 You have 35 minutes to complete this test. Use the answer sheets in the back of the book to mark your answers.

Here is the Table of Contents from *Deserts,* a book Joan found in the library. Study the Table of Contents carefully. Then answer questions 6–9.

## Table of Contents

6    Chapter 5 contains information on all of these *except*—

F    insects of the desert.

G    the prickly pear cactus.

H    the desert rose.

J    date palm trees.

7    On which page should Joan start reading to find out how the camel survives in the desert?

A    18

B    22

C    27

D    34

8    Which chapter should Joan read to learn about animals living in the desert?

_____

_____

_____

_____

9    Which chapter would have information about how deserts get water?

F    Chapter 2

G    Chapter 4

H    Chapter 5

J    Chapter 7

Before starting her report, Joan looked up several words in the dictionary.

10    The "a" in *locate* sounds most like the vowel sound in—

A    sand.

B    lake.

C    fair.

D    large

GO ON

Here is a rough draft of the first part of Joan's report. Read the rough draft carefully. Then answer questions 11–16.

---

# A Dry Land

When you think of a desert, what do you think of? You probably
(1)                                                              (2)

think of a place that is hot all the time. Some deserts are hot all the
(3)

time. But there are deserts that are found in cold places. What makes a
(4)                                                              (5)

place a desert is not how hot or cold it is there. What makes it a desert
(6)

is how much rain it gets. A desert is a place. That gets less than 10
(7)                                    (8)

inches of rain a year.

Because there are no clouds to protect the ground, the days in some
(9)

deserts are warm. At night there are no clouds to keep the heat from
(10)

leaving the ground. The Sahara is a large desert in Africa. So the
(11)                                                              (12)

nights in a desert get very cold. Strong winds can be found in most
(13)

deserts. There are very few plants and trees to slow down the winds.
(14)

So the winds can easily pick up the sand and create sandstorms.
(15)

---

GO ON

**11** Which sentence best combines sentences 3 and 4 without changing their meaning?

F Although some deserts are hot all the time, there are deserts that are found in cold places.

G Some deserts are hot, there are deserts that are found in cold.

H There are deserts that are found in cold places, some deserts are hot all the time.

J Some deserts are hot all the time, there are deserts that are cold.

**12** Which sentence does *not belong* in the second paragraph? Write its number.

_____

_____

_____

_____

**13** Which group of words is *not* a complete sentence?

A 8

B 9

C 10

D 11

**14** What is the most colorful way to write sentence 12?

F So it can be very cold in the night in a desert.

G So it can often become quite cold in a desert during the night.

H So the nights in a desert can be very cold.

J As it is written.

**15** The best way to write sentence 13 is—

A There are strong winds to be found in most deserts.

B Strong winds in most deserts can be found.

C In most deserts can be found strong winds.

D As it is written.

**16** Which of these sentences could be added after sentence 15?

F Many kinds of animals live in the world's deserts.

G The Atacama Desert is found in South America.

H What do you think it would be like to live in a desert?

J Sometimes the blowing sand can be so thick that it is hard to see in front of you.

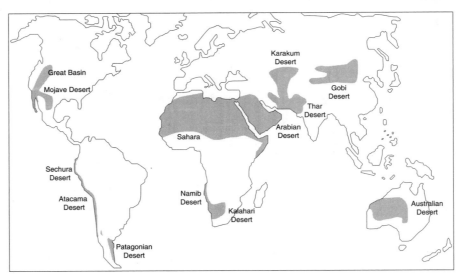

**Here is the next part of Joan's rough draft for her report. This part has certain words and phrases underlined. Read the draft carefully. Then answer questions 17–26.**

Camels are important animals of the desert. They is used to carry
(16)                                                          (17)

people and goods through the sunny dry, and windy desert. Camels can
                                                    (18)

survive the heat and dryness of the desert.

The camel's body helps the camel live in the desert! The camel has
(19)                                    (20)

long eyelashes that keep the sand out of its eyes. The camel can keep his
                                                                    (21)

eyes closed and see well enough through its thin eyelids. The fur in an
                                                                    (22)

camel's ears also helps to keep sand from getting in. The long legs of a
(23)

camel keep their body higher off the ground, where the air is cool more.

The camel eats tough desert plants. It can go for many days without
(24)                                    (25)

food. The camels' humps store fat. The camel can use this fat when it
         (26)                                    (27)

does'nt have enough to eat. Although the camel can go for days without
                                    (28)

water, it does need water to live. A camel can drink up to 18 gallons of
                                    (29)

water at one time.

---

**17**  **In sentence 17, They is used is best written—**

   **A**  They used

   **B**  They are used

   **C**  They were used

   **D**  As it is written.

**18**  **In sentence 17, the sunny dry, and windy desert is best written—**

   **F**  the sunny dry and windy desert

   **G**  the sunny, dry, and windy, desert

   **H**  the sunny, dry, and windy desert

   **J**  As it is written.

GO ON

**19**  In sentence 19, <u>live in the desert!</u> is best written—

    **A**  live in the desert.

    **B**  lives in the desert!

    **C**  live in the desert?

    **D**  As it is written.

**20**  In sentence 21, <u>keep his eyes</u> is best written—

    **F**  keep their eyes

    **G**  keep its eyes

    **H**  keep it eyes

    **J**  As it is written.

**21**  In sentence 22, <u>an camel's ears</u> is best written—

    **A**  an Camel's ears

    **B**  an camels ears

    **C**  a camel's ears

    **D**  As it is written.

**22**  In sentence 23, <u>keep their body</u> is best written—

    **F**  keep its body

    **G**  keep them body

    **H**  keep his body

    **J**  As it is written.

**23**  In sentence 23, <u>air is cool more</u> is best written—

    **A**  air is most cool

    **B**  air is cooler

    **C**  air is more cooler

    **D**  As it is written.

**24**  In sentence 25, <u>It can go</u> is best written—

    **F**  It gone

    **G**  It went

    **H**  It can went

    **J**  As it is written.

**25**  In sentence 26, <u>camels' humps</u> is best written—

    **A**  camels humps

    **B**  camel's humps

    **C**  camel humps

    **D**  As it is written.

**26**  In sentence 27, <u>when it does'nt have enough</u> is best written—

    **F**  when it doesnt' have enough

    **G**  when it doesnt have enough

    **H**  when it doesn't have enough

    **J**  As it is written.

GO ON

For questions 27–38, read each sentence carefully. If one of the words is misspelled, darken the circle for that word. If all of the words are spelled correctly, then darken the circle for *No mistake*.

27    Darren and Jamie left <u>immediatly</u> <u>following</u> the <u>concert</u>. <u>No mistake</u>
                              A            B              C            D

28    I would like to <u>exshange</u> this <u>shirt</u> for a <u>larger</u> one. <u>No mistake</u>
                        F              G            H                 J

29    Roy <u>received</u> <u>permision</u> to <u>drive</u> his father's car. <u>No mistake</u>
            A            B             C                          D

30    Marta and her <u>brothers</u> collect <u>aluminum</u> cans to <u>recycle</u>. <u>No mistake</u>
                     F                  G                  H              J

31    The <u>messenger</u> was <u>carrying</u> important <u>imformation</u>. <u>No mistake</u>
            A             B                 C                D

32    Lin <u>through</u> the <u>pebble</u> into the <u>pond</u>. <u>No mistake</u>
            F             G              H           J

33    It would be a good <u>idea</u> to <u>obtane</u> your <u>tickets</u> before the show. <u>No mistake</u>
                          A           B            C                             D

34    The <u>sponge</u> <u>absorbed</u> the water <u>completely</u>. <u>No mistake</u>
            F           G                    H              J

35    Manuel was <u>eraseing</u> the <u>chalkboard</u> after <u>class</u>. <u>No mistake</u>
                  A                B                  C            D

36    She <u>adjustted</u> the <u>television</u> to get a clear <u>picture</u>. <u>No mistake</u>
            F                G                         H             J

37    We <u>climbed</u> over the <u>bolder</u> to reach the <u>entrance</u> to the cave. <u>No mistake</u>
           A                 B                   C                              D

38    <u>During</u> the seventeenth <u>century</u>, Spain had many <u>colonys</u>. <u>No mistake</u>
         F                       G                        H           J

STOP

125

# Core Skills: Test Preparation, Grade 4
## Answer Key

**Unit 2: Page 7**
1. B
2. J
3. not liked
4. A

**Page 8**
1. D
2. F
3. B
4. cave

**Pages 9–10**
1. B
2. G
3. eats
4. A
5. F
6. connected

**Page 11**
1. C
2. the tide
3. F
4. D

**Page 12**
1. C
2. after the mahouts tie a short rope to the chain
3. H

**Page 13**
1. A
2. after he examined all the wheels carefully

**Page 14**
1. B
2. J
3. B
4. May 1, 1893

**Page 15**
1. B
2. H
3. C
4. how to remove gum from clothes

**Page 16**
1. D
2. G
3. Jackie Cochran was a natural pilot.

**Pages 17–18**
1. A
2. why people started saying "bless you" when someone sneezes
3. G
4. why the feathers on flamingos are bright pink

**Pages 19–20**
1. C
2. J
3. they need to hide from enemies
4. C
5. G
6. B
7. fish can't live in its salty water

**Pages 21–22**
1. B
2. A
3. She will scold Andres and Nicole because they forgot to turn off the water when they were finished.
4. B
5. A
6. dip a brush into the paint and start painting

**Pages 23–24**
1. A
2. Monday
3. J
4. Mexico was under Spanish rule for 300 years.

**Pages 25–26**
1. A
2. G
3. October. The clue was in the last sentence that stated that Reggie Jackson was known as Mr. October.
4. B
5. H
6. He thought all the continents were once a large land mass that had drifted apart over time.

**Pages 27–28**
1. A
2. F
3. He feels his son should wait until he finishes school to take a job.
4. A
5. He is very nervous about flying.

**Pages 29–30**
1. C
2. F
3. D
4. G
5. B

**Unit 3: Pages 31–38**
**Sample A: C**
1. D
2. to escape from their enemies
3. H
4. A
5. by reading a newspaper story about how President Roosevelt saved a small bear cub on a hunting trip
6. J
7. B
8. J
9. A
10. F
11. C
12. J
13. A
14. several days
15. a week
16. H
17. A
18. G
19. Earth Patrol
20. A
21. H
22. C
23. J
24. D
25. G
26. D
27. H
28. D
29. the fawn
30. J
31. D
32. F

**Pages 39–45**
**Sample A: B**
1. B
2. H
3. C
4. to protect it from wild animals
5. J
6. A
7. H
8. to stay safe
9. B
10. H
11. A
12. F
13. C

14. G
15. B
16. H
17. A
18. G
19. C
20. continue to swallow its prey
21. J
22. A
23. fourth graders at Main Street School
24. J
25. C
26. J
27. B
28. H

**Unit 4: Page 46**
**Sample A: D**
1. D
2. G
3. B
4. H
5. D
6. H
7. C
8. G

**Page 47**
**Sample A: D**
1. B
2. G
3. C
4. G

**Page 48**
**Sample A: A**
1. A
2. J
3. C
4. G
5. B
6. empty

**Pages 49–51**
**Sample A: D**
1. D
2. H
3. D
4. J
5. C
6. G
7. B
8. F
9. a mistake
**Sample B: D**
10. D
11. H
12. B
13. F
14. B

**Sample C: C**
15. H
16. B
17. F
18. C
19. G
20. C
21. J
22. A

**Unit 5: Page 53**
**Step 1:** to determine if Jason has enough money for both purchases

**Step 2:** CDs cost $14.99 each. Cassette tapes cost $9.99 each. Jason has $23.00.

**Step 3:** Estimate the cost of the two items.

**Step 4:**
  Just under $15
+ Just under $10
  Just under $25

$23.00 Does not have enough to buy both items.

**Step 5:** Yes, because the actual sum of the prices of each item must be greater than $23.

**Page 54**
**Step 1:** to use the bills Mr. Johnson has to make exactly $38

**Step 2:**
2-20s   4-5s
3-10s   4-1s

**Step 3:** Try different combinations until the sum of 38 is obtained.

**Step 4:**
20 + 10 + 5 + 3 = $38
Bills consisting of 1 twenty, 1 ten, 1 five, and 3 ones would make exactly $38.

**Step 5:** The solution is acceptable because $38 was obtained using the money available.

**Unit 6: Page 55**
**Sample A: A**
1. C
2. F
3. D
4. 10

**Page 56**
**Sample A: C**
1. D
2. G
3. A
4. 2
5. J

**Pages 57–58**
**Sample A: C**
1. 3,800
2. C
3. G
4. New York and Pennsylvania
5. A
6. J
7. D
8. F

**Pages 59–60**
**Sample A: C**
1. D
2. H
3. A
4. J
5. rectangle
6. A
7. H
8. B
9. F
10. 5

**Pages 61–62**
**Sample A: C**
1. A
2. G
3. B
4. J
5. A
6. F
7. B
8. H
9. C

**Page 63**
**Sample A: B**
1. C
2. G
3. C
4. 69

**Page 64**
**Sample A: B**
1. C
2. 900
3. G
4. B

**Page 65**
**Sample A: B**
1. A
2. pizza
3. H
4. D

**Page 66**
**Sample A: C**
1. E
2. 683
3. G
4. D
5. H
6. A

**Page 67**
**Sample A: B**
1. D
2. J
3. C
4. K

**Pages 68–70**
**Sample A: C**
**Sample B: H**
1. C
2. K
3. C
4. 374
5. K
6. B
7. F
8. A
9. J
10. $4.77
11. H
12. H
13. C
14. G
15. C
16. G
17. C
18. K
19. A
20. 6 inches
21. F
22. B

**Pages 71–76**
**Sample A: C**
1. D
2. G
3. three-thousand four-hundred sixty
4. D
5. F
6. A
7. G
8. D
9. F
10. B
11. Buster
12. G
13. C
14. G
15. A
16. F
17. D
18. G
19. pie
20. D
21. H
22. D
23. square
24. F
25. B
26. F
27. 5 cm
28. B
29. J
30. B
31. H
32. A
33. F
34. A
35. 44
36. G

**Unit 7: Page 77**
**Sample A: C**
1. A
2. H
3. A
4. F
5. D
6. F
7. A
8. H
9. A
10. J

**Page 78**
**Sample A: C**
1. A
2. J
3. B
4. H
5. C
6. F
7. A
8. J
9. C
10. F
11. C
12. G

**Pages 79–80**
**Sample A: C**
1. A
2. H
3. C
4. H
5. A
6. G
7. B
8. F
9. B
10. G
11. B
12. F
13. A
**Sample B: C**
14. G
15. B
16. F
17. D
18. J
19. B
20. J
21. A
22. H
23. C
24. G
25. C

**Unit 8: Pages 81–86**
**Sample A: C**
1. D
2. J
3. A
4. 106–108
5. J
6. C
7. G
8. B
9. J
10. C
11. F
12. B
13. 9
14. G
15. A
16. H
17. D
18. G
19. A
20. F
21. C
22. F

**Page 87**
**Sample A: A**
1. D
2. G
3. A
4. F
5. D
6. G
7. A
8. H

**Pages 88–93**
**Sample A: B**
1. A
2. G
3. B
4. J
5. 4
6. D
7. H
8. B
9. G
10. C
11. G
12. C
13. H
14. C
15. F
16. B
17. J
18. A
19. G
20. A
21. F
22. D
23. H
24. A
25. G
26. D
27. G
28. A
29. F
30. C

**Pages 94–125**
See pages 129 and 130 for the multiple-choice answers.

**Comprehensive Tests: Open-Ended Answers**
**Page 95**
6. 18 feet long

**Page 97**
12. because he couldn't think of anything to write about

**Page 99**
25. to make it thin out evenly

**Page 101**
32. She had to take classes at Hull House to learn English and about the American way of life, as well as about the government of the United States.

**Page 103**
41. the Rose Hotel

**Page 108**
8. two thousand six hundred five
9. 7

**Page 109**
18. Green Thumb Hour

**Page 110**
21. 3 inches

**Page 111**
32. $0.51

**Page 113**
42. 7 inches

**Page 114**
45. 2

**Page 115**
8. 4

**Page 116**
12. 1

**Page 120**
8. 6

**Page 122**
12. 11

# Answer Sheet

**STUDENT'S NAME**

**LAST** | **FIRST** | **MI**

**SCHOOL:**

**TEACHER:**

FEMALE ○    MALE ○

**BIRTH DATE**

| Jan ○ | ⓪ | ⓪ | ⓪ | ⓪ |
| Feb ○ | ① | ① | ① | ① |
| Mar ○ | ② | ② | ② | ② |
| Apr ○ | ③ | ③ | ③ | ③ |
| May ○ | | ④ | ④ | ④ |
| Jun ○ | | ⑤ | ⑤ | ⑤ |
| Jul ○ | | ⑥ | ⑥ | ⑥ |
| Aug ○ | | ⑦ | ⑦ | ⑦ |
| Sep ○ | | ⑧ | ⑧ | ⑧ |
| Oct ○ | | ⑨ | ⑨ | ⑨ |
| Nov ○ | | | | |
| Dec ○ | | | | |

**GRADE** ④ ⑤ ⑥ ⑦ ⑧

*Core Skills:*
*Test Preparation*
# Grade 4
© Steck-Vaughn Company

(Name grid columns A–Z)

## TEST 1    Reading Comprehension

**SA** Ⓐ Ⓑ ● Ⓓ
1  Ⓐ ● Ⓒ Ⓓ
2  Ⓕ Ⓖ Ⓗ ●
3  Ⓐ Ⓑ ● Ⓓ
4  Ⓕ Ⓖ ● Ⓙ
5  ● Ⓑ Ⓒ Ⓓ
6  **OPEN ENDED**
7  ● Ⓖ Ⓗ Ⓙ

8  Ⓐ Ⓑ Ⓒ ●
9  Ⓕ ● Ⓗ Ⓙ
10 Ⓐ Ⓑ ● Ⓓ
11 Ⓕ Ⓖ Ⓗ ●
12 **OPEN ENDED**
13 Ⓐ ● Ⓒ Ⓓ
14 Ⓕ Ⓖ ● Ⓙ
15 Ⓐ Ⓑ ● Ⓓ

16 Ⓕ Ⓖ ● Ⓙ
17 Ⓐ Ⓑ Ⓒ ●
18 Ⓕ Ⓖ ● Ⓙ
19 Ⓐ ● Ⓒ Ⓓ
20 ● Ⓖ Ⓗ Ⓙ
21 ● Ⓑ Ⓒ Ⓓ
22 Ⓕ Ⓖ Ⓗ ●
23 Ⓐ Ⓑ Ⓒ ●

24 Ⓕ Ⓖ ● Ⓙ
25 **OPEN ENDED**
26 Ⓐ Ⓑ ● Ⓓ
27 Ⓕ Ⓖ ● Ⓙ
28 Ⓐ Ⓑ Ⓒ ●
29 ● Ⓖ Ⓗ Ⓙ
30 Ⓐ Ⓑ Ⓒ ●
31 ● Ⓖ Ⓗ Ⓙ

32 **OPEN ENDED**
33 Ⓐ Ⓑ Ⓒ ●
34 Ⓕ Ⓖ ● Ⓙ
35 Ⓐ Ⓑ ● Ⓓ
36 Ⓕ ● Ⓗ Ⓙ
37 Ⓐ ● Ⓒ Ⓓ
38 Ⓕ Ⓖ ● Ⓙ
39 ● Ⓑ Ⓒ Ⓓ

40 Ⓕ ● Ⓗ Ⓙ
41 **OPEN ENDED**
42 ● Ⓑ Ⓒ Ⓓ
43 ● Ⓖ Ⓗ Ⓙ
44 Ⓐ Ⓑ ● Ⓓ
45 Ⓕ Ⓖ Ⓗ ●
46 Ⓐ Ⓑ ● Ⓓ

## TEST 2    Reading Vocabulary

**SA** Ⓐ Ⓑ ● Ⓓ
1  ● Ⓑ Ⓒ Ⓓ
2  Ⓕ ● Ⓗ Ⓙ
3  Ⓐ Ⓑ ● Ⓓ
4  Ⓕ ● Ⓗ Ⓙ

5  Ⓐ ● Ⓒ Ⓓ
6  Ⓕ Ⓖ ● Ⓙ
7  ● Ⓑ Ⓒ Ⓓ
8  Ⓕ Ⓖ Ⓗ ●
9  Ⓐ ● Ⓒ Ⓓ

**SB** Ⓐ Ⓑ Ⓒ ●
10 ● Ⓖ Ⓗ Ⓙ
11 Ⓐ Ⓑ ● Ⓓ
12 Ⓕ ● Ⓗ Ⓙ
13 Ⓐ Ⓑ Ⓒ ●

14 ● Ⓖ Ⓗ Ⓙ
**SC** Ⓐ ● Ⓒ Ⓓ
15 Ⓐ Ⓑ ● Ⓓ
16 Ⓕ Ⓖ Ⓗ ●
17 Ⓐ ● Ⓒ Ⓓ

18 ● Ⓖ Ⓗ Ⓙ
19 Ⓐ ● Ⓒ Ⓓ
20 Ⓕ Ⓖ Ⓗ ●
21 Ⓐ ● Ⓒ Ⓓ
22 Ⓕ Ⓖ ● Ⓙ

# TEST 3     Part 1: Math Problem Solving

- SA (A) (B) (C) **●(D)**
- 1 **●(A)** (B) (C) (D)
- 2 (F) **●(G)** (H) (J)
- 3 **●(A)** (B) (C) (D)
- 4 (F) (G) (H) **●(J)**
- 5 (A) (B) **●(C)** (D)
- 6 (F) **●(G)** (H) (J)
- 7 (A) (B) (C) **●(D)**
- 8 OPEN ENDED
- 9 OPEN ENDED
- 10 **●(F)** (G) (H) (J)
- 11 (A) (B) **●(C)** (D)
- 12 (F) (G) **●(H)** (J)
- 13 (A) (B) (C) **●(D)**
- 14 **●(F)** (G) (H) (J)
- 15 (A) (B) (C) **●(D)**
- 16 (F) (G) (H) **●(J)**
- 17 (A) (B) **●(C)** (D)
- 18 OPEN ENDED
- 19 (F) (G) (H) **●(J)**
- 20 (A) **●(B)** (C) (D)
- 21 OPEN ENDED
- 22 (F) (G) (H) **●(J)**
- 23 (A) (B) **●(C)** (D)
- 24 (F) **●(G)** (H) (J)
- 25 **●(A)** (B) (C) (D)
- 26 (F) **●(G)** (H) (J)
- 27 **●(A)** (B) (C) (D)
- 28 **●(F)** (G) (H) (J)
- 29 (A) (B) **●(C)** (D)
- 30 (F) (G) (H) **●(J)**
- 31 (A) **●(B)** (C) (D)
- 32 OPEN ENDED
- 33 (F) (G) (H) **●(J)**
- 34 (A) **●(B)** (C) (D)
- 35 (F) (G) (H) **●(J)**
- 36 **●(A)** (B) (C) (D)
- 37 (F) (G) (H) **●(J)**
- 38 (A) (B) **●(C)** (D)
- 39 **●(F)** (G) (H) (J)
- 40 **●(A)** (B) (C) (D)
- 41 (F) (G) (H) **●(J)**
- 42 OPEN ENDED
- 43 (A) (B) (C) **●(D)**
- 44 (F) (G) **●(H)** (J)
- 45 OPEN ENDED
- 46 (A) **●(B)** (C) (D)
- 47 (F) **●(G)** (H) (J)
- 48 (A) (B) **●(C)** (D)
- 49 (F) (G) (H) **●(J)**

## Part 2: Math Procedures

- SA (A) (B) (C) **●(D)** (E)
- 1 (A) **●(B)** (C) (D) (E)
- 2 **●(F)** (G) (H) (J) (K)
- 3 (A) (B) **●(C)** (D) (E)
- 4 (F) (G) (H) **●(J)** (K)
- 5 (A) **●(B)** (C) (D) (E)
- 6 (F) **●(G)** (H) (J) (K)
- 7 (A) (B) (C) **●(D)** (E)
- 8 OPEN ENDED
- 9 (F) **●(G)** (H) (J) (K)
- 10 (A) (B) **●(C)** (D) (E)
- 11 **●(F)** (G) (H) (J) (K)
- 12 OPEN ENDED
- 13 (A) (B) **●(C)** (D) (E)
- 14 (F) **●(G)** (H) (J) (K)
- 15 (A) (B) (C) (D) **●(E)**
- SB (A) (B) (C) **●(D)** (E)

# TEST 4     Listening

- SA **●(A)** (B) (C) (D)
- 1 **●(A)** (B) (C) (D)
- 2 **●(F)** (G) (H) (J)
- 3 (A) **●(B)** (C) (D)
- 4 (F) **●(G)** (H) (J)
- 5 (A) (B) (C) **●(D)**
- 6 (F) **●(G)** (H) (J)
- 7 (A) **●(B)** (C) (D)
- 8 (F) (G) (H) **●(J)**
- 9 (A) (B) **●(C)** (D)
- 10 (F) (G) (H) **●(J)**
- 11 (A) (B) **●(C)** (D)
- 12 **●(F)** (G) (H) (J)
- 13 **●(A)** (B) (C) (D)
- 14 **●(F)** (G) (H) (J)
- 15 (A) (B) **●(C)** (D)
- 16 **●(F)** (G) (H) (J)
- 17 **●(A)** (B) (C) (D)
- 18 (F) **●(G)** (H) (J)
- 19 (A) **●(B)** (C) (D)
- 20 (F) (G) (H) **●(J)**
- 21 (A) **●(B)** (C) (D)
- 22 (F) (G) (H) **●(J)**
- 23 **●(A)** (B) (C) (D)
- SB (A) **●(B)** (C) (D)
- 24 (F) **●(G)** (H) (J)
- 25 (A) (B) **●(C)** (D)

# TEST 5     Language

- SA (A) **●(B)** (C) (D)
- 1 (A) (B) (C) **●(D)**
- 2 (F) **●(G)** (H) (J)
- 3 (A) (B) (C) **●(D)**
- 4 **●(F)** (G) (H) (J)
- 5 (A) (B) (C) **●(D)**
- 6 **●(F)** (G) (H) (J)
- 7 (A) (B) (C) **●(D)**
- 8 OPEN ENDED
- 9 (F) **●(G)** (H) (J)
- 10 (A) **●(B)** (C) (D)
- 11 **●(F)** (G) (H) (J)
- 12 OPEN ENDED
- 13 **●(A)** (B) (C) (D)
- 14 (F) (G) (H) **●(J)**
- 15 (A) (B) (C) **●(D)**
- 16 (F) (G) (H) **●(J)**
- 17 (A) **●(B)** (C) (D)
- 18 (F) (G) **●(H)** (J)
- 19 **●(A)** (B) (C) (D)
- 20 (F) **●(G)** (H) (J)
- 21 (A) (B) **●(C)** (D)
- 22 **●(F)** (G) (H) (J)
- 23 (A) **●(B)** (C) (D)
- 24 (F) (G) (H) **●(J)**
- 25 (A) **●(B)** (C) (D)
- 26 (F) (G) **●(H)** (J)
- 27 **●(A)** (B) (C) (D)
- 28 **●(F)** (G) (H) (J)
- 29 (A) **●(B)** (C) (D)
- 30 (F) (G) **●(H)** (J)
- 31 (A) (B) **●(C)** (D)
- 32 **●(F)** (G) (H) (J)
- 33 (A) **●(B)** (C) (D)
- 34 (F) (G) (H) **●(J)**
- 35 **●(A)** (B) (C) (D)
- 36 **●(F)** (G) (H) (J)
- 37 (A) **●(B)** (C) (D)
- 38 (F) (G) **●(H)** (J)

# Answer Sheet

**STUDENT'S NAME**

LAST | FIRST | MI

**SCHOOL:**

**TEACHER:**

FEMALE ○    MALE ○

*(name grid with bubbles A–Z for each letter column)*

**BIRTH DATE**

| MONTH | DAY | | YEAR | |
|---|---|---|---|---|
| Jan ○ | ⓪ | ⓪ | ⓪ | ⓪ |
| Feb ○ | ① | ① | ① | ① |
| Mar ○ | ② | ② | ② | ② |
| Apr ○ | ③ | ③ | ③ | ③ |
| May ○ | | ④ | ④ | ④ |
| Jun ○ | | ⑤ | ⑤ | ⑤ |
| Jul ○ | | ⑥ | ⑥ | ⑥ |
| Aug ○ | | ⑦ | ⑦ | ⑦ |
| Sep ○ | | ⑧ | ⑧ | ⑧ |
| Oct ○ | | ⑨ | ⑨ | ⑨ |
| Nov ○ | | | | |
| Dec ○ | | | | |

**GRADE** ④ ⑤ ⑥ ⑦ ⑧

## Core Skills:
### Test Preparation
# Grade 4

© Steck-Vaughn Company

---

**TEST 1    Reading Comprehension**

SA ⒶⒷⒸⒹ    8 ⒶⒷⒸⒹ    16 ⒻⒼⒽⒿ    24 ⒻⒼⒽⒿ    32 OPEN ENDED    40 ⒻⒼⒽⒿ
1 ⒶⒷⒸⒹ    9 ⒻⒼⒽⒿ    17 ⒶⒷⒸⒹ    25 OPEN ENDED    33 ⒶⒷⒸⒹ    41 OPEN ENDED
2 ⒻⒼⒽⒿ    10 ⒶⒷⒸⒹ    18 ⒻⒼⒽⒿ    26 ⒶⒷⒸⒹ    34 ⒻⒼⒽⒿ    42 ⒶⒷⒸⒹ
3 ⒶⒷⒸⒹ    11 ⒻⒼⒽⒿ    19 ⒶⒷⒸⒹ    27 ⒻⒼⒽⒿ    35 ⒶⒷⒸⒹ    43 ⒻⒼⒽⒿ
4 ⒻⒼⒽⒿ    12 OPEN ENDED    20 ⒻⒼⒽⒿ    28 ⒶⒷⒸⒹ    36 ⒻⒼⒽⒿ    44 ⒶⒷⒸⒹ
5 ⒶⒷⒸⒹ    13 ⒶⒷⒸⒹ    21 ⒶⒷⒸⒹ    29 ⒻⒼⒽⒿ    37 ⒶⒷⒸⒹ    45 ⒻⒼⒽⒿ
6 OPEN ENDED    14 ⒻⒼⒽⒿ    22 ⒻⒼⒽⒿ    30 ⒶⒷⒸⒹ    38 ⒻⒼⒽⒿ    46 ⒶⒷⒸⒹ
7 ⒻⒼⒽⒿ    15 ⒶⒷⒸⒹ    23 ⒶⒷⒸⒹ    31 ⒻⒼⒽⒿ    39 ⒶⒷⒸⒹ

---

**TEST 2    Reading Vocabulary**

SA ⒶⒷⒸⒹ    5 ⒶⒷⒸⒹ    SB ⒶⒷⒸⒹ    14 ⒻⒼⒽⒿ    18 ⒻⒼⒽⒿ
1 ⒶⒷⒸⒹ    6 ⒻⒼⒽⒿ    10 ⒻⒼⒽⒿ    SC ⒶⒷⒸⒹ    19 ⒶⒷⒸⒹ
2 ⒻⒼⒽⒿ    7 ⒶⒷⒸⒹ    11 ⒶⒷⒸⒹ    15 ⒶⒷⒸⒹ    20 ⒻⒼⒽⒿ
3 ⒶⒷⒸⒹ    8 ⒻⒼⒽⒿ    12 ⒻⒼⒽⒿ    16 ⒻⒼⒽⒿ    21 ⒶⒷⒸⒹ
4 ⒻⒼⒽⒿ    9 ⒶⒷⒸⒹ    13 ⒶⒷⒸⒹ    17 ⒶⒷⒸⒹ    22 ⒻⒼⒽⒿ

CUT HERE

# TEST 3 — Part 1: Math Problem Solving

SA Ⓐ Ⓑ Ⓒ Ⓓ

1 Ⓐ Ⓑ Ⓒ Ⓓ
2 Ⓕ Ⓖ Ⓗ Ⓙ
3 Ⓐ Ⓑ Ⓒ Ⓓ
4 Ⓕ Ⓖ Ⓗ Ⓙ
5 Ⓐ Ⓑ Ⓒ Ⓓ
6 Ⓕ Ⓖ Ⓗ Ⓙ
7 Ⓐ Ⓑ Ⓒ Ⓓ
8 OPEN ENDED

9 OPEN ENDED
10 Ⓕ Ⓖ Ⓗ Ⓙ
11 Ⓐ Ⓑ Ⓒ Ⓓ
12 Ⓕ Ⓖ Ⓗ Ⓙ
13 Ⓐ Ⓑ Ⓒ Ⓓ
14 Ⓕ Ⓖ Ⓗ Ⓙ
15 Ⓐ Ⓑ Ⓒ Ⓓ
16 Ⓕ Ⓖ Ⓗ Ⓙ
17 Ⓐ Ⓑ Ⓒ Ⓓ

18 OPEN ENDED
19 Ⓕ Ⓖ Ⓗ Ⓙ
20 Ⓐ Ⓑ Ⓒ Ⓓ
21 OPEN ENDED
22 Ⓕ Ⓖ Ⓗ Ⓙ
23 Ⓐ Ⓑ Ⓒ Ⓓ
24 Ⓕ Ⓖ Ⓗ Ⓙ
25 Ⓐ Ⓑ Ⓒ Ⓓ
26 Ⓕ Ⓖ Ⓗ Ⓙ

27 Ⓐ Ⓑ Ⓒ Ⓓ
28 Ⓕ Ⓖ Ⓗ Ⓙ
29 Ⓐ Ⓑ Ⓒ Ⓓ
30 Ⓕ Ⓖ Ⓗ Ⓙ
31 Ⓐ Ⓑ Ⓒ Ⓓ
32 OPEN ENDED
33 Ⓕ Ⓖ Ⓗ Ⓙ
34 Ⓐ Ⓑ Ⓒ Ⓓ
35 Ⓕ Ⓖ Ⓗ Ⓙ

36 Ⓐ Ⓑ Ⓒ Ⓓ
37 Ⓕ Ⓖ Ⓗ Ⓙ
38 Ⓐ Ⓑ Ⓒ Ⓓ
39 Ⓕ Ⓖ Ⓗ Ⓙ
40 Ⓐ Ⓑ Ⓒ Ⓓ
41 Ⓕ Ⓖ Ⓗ Ⓙ
42 OPEN ENDED
43 Ⓐ Ⓑ Ⓒ Ⓓ
44 Ⓕ Ⓖ Ⓗ Ⓙ

45 OPEN ENDED
46 Ⓐ Ⓑ Ⓒ Ⓓ
47 Ⓕ Ⓖ Ⓗ Ⓙ
48 Ⓐ Ⓑ Ⓒ Ⓓ
49 Ⓕ Ⓖ Ⓗ Ⓙ

## Part 2: Math Procedures

SA Ⓐ Ⓑ Ⓒ Ⓓ Ⓔ

1 Ⓐ Ⓑ Ⓒ Ⓓ Ⓔ
2 Ⓕ Ⓖ Ⓗ Ⓙ Ⓚ

3 Ⓐ Ⓑ Ⓒ Ⓓ Ⓔ
4 Ⓕ Ⓖ Ⓗ Ⓙ Ⓚ
5 Ⓐ Ⓑ Ⓒ Ⓓ Ⓔ

6 Ⓕ Ⓖ Ⓗ Ⓙ Ⓚ
7 Ⓐ Ⓑ Ⓒ Ⓓ Ⓔ
8 OPEN ENDED

9 Ⓕ Ⓖ Ⓗ Ⓙ Ⓚ
SB Ⓐ Ⓑ Ⓒ Ⓓ Ⓔ
10 Ⓐ Ⓑ Ⓒ Ⓓ Ⓔ

11 Ⓕ Ⓖ Ⓗ Ⓙ Ⓚ
12 OPEN ENDED
13 Ⓐ Ⓑ Ⓒ Ⓓ Ⓔ

14 Ⓕ Ⓖ Ⓗ Ⓙ Ⓚ
15 Ⓐ Ⓑ Ⓒ Ⓓ Ⓔ

# TEST 4 — Listening

SA Ⓐ Ⓑ Ⓒ Ⓓ

1 Ⓐ Ⓑ Ⓒ Ⓓ
2 Ⓕ Ⓖ Ⓗ Ⓙ
3 Ⓐ Ⓑ Ⓒ Ⓓ
4 Ⓕ Ⓖ Ⓗ Ⓙ

5 Ⓐ Ⓑ Ⓒ Ⓓ
6 Ⓕ Ⓖ Ⓗ Ⓙ
7 Ⓐ Ⓑ Ⓒ Ⓓ
8 Ⓕ Ⓖ Ⓗ Ⓙ
9 Ⓐ Ⓑ Ⓒ Ⓓ

10 Ⓕ Ⓖ Ⓗ Ⓙ
11 Ⓐ Ⓑ Ⓒ Ⓓ
12 Ⓕ Ⓖ Ⓗ Ⓙ
13 Ⓐ Ⓑ Ⓒ Ⓓ
SB Ⓐ Ⓑ Ⓒ Ⓓ

14 Ⓕ Ⓖ Ⓗ Ⓙ
15 Ⓐ Ⓑ Ⓒ Ⓓ
16 Ⓕ Ⓖ Ⓗ Ⓙ
17 Ⓐ Ⓑ Ⓒ Ⓓ
18 Ⓕ Ⓖ Ⓗ Ⓙ

19 Ⓐ Ⓑ Ⓒ Ⓓ
20 Ⓕ Ⓖ Ⓗ Ⓙ
21 Ⓐ Ⓑ Ⓒ Ⓓ
22 Ⓕ Ⓖ Ⓗ Ⓙ
23 Ⓐ Ⓑ Ⓒ Ⓓ

24 Ⓕ Ⓖ Ⓗ Ⓙ
25 Ⓐ Ⓑ Ⓒ Ⓓ

# TEST 5 — Language

SA Ⓐ Ⓑ Ⓒ Ⓓ

1 Ⓐ Ⓑ Ⓒ Ⓓ
2 Ⓕ Ⓖ Ⓗ Ⓙ
3 Ⓐ Ⓑ Ⓒ Ⓓ
4 Ⓕ Ⓖ Ⓗ Ⓙ
5 Ⓐ Ⓑ Ⓒ Ⓓ
6 Ⓕ Ⓖ Ⓗ Ⓙ

7 Ⓐ Ⓑ Ⓒ Ⓓ
8 OPEN ENDED
9 Ⓕ Ⓖ Ⓗ Ⓙ
10 Ⓐ Ⓑ Ⓒ Ⓓ
11 Ⓕ Ⓖ Ⓗ Ⓙ
12 OPEN ENDED
13 Ⓐ Ⓑ Ⓒ Ⓓ

14 Ⓕ Ⓖ Ⓗ Ⓙ
15 Ⓐ Ⓑ Ⓒ Ⓓ
16 Ⓕ Ⓖ Ⓗ Ⓙ
17 Ⓐ Ⓑ Ⓒ Ⓓ
18 Ⓕ Ⓖ Ⓗ Ⓙ
19 Ⓐ Ⓑ Ⓒ Ⓓ
20 Ⓕ Ⓖ Ⓗ Ⓙ

21 Ⓐ Ⓑ Ⓒ Ⓓ
22 Ⓕ Ⓖ Ⓗ Ⓙ
23 Ⓐ Ⓑ Ⓒ Ⓓ
24 Ⓕ Ⓖ Ⓗ Ⓙ
25 Ⓐ Ⓑ Ⓒ Ⓓ
26 Ⓕ Ⓖ Ⓗ Ⓙ
27 Ⓐ Ⓑ Ⓒ Ⓓ

28 Ⓕ Ⓖ Ⓗ Ⓙ
29 Ⓐ Ⓑ Ⓒ Ⓓ
30 Ⓕ Ⓖ Ⓗ Ⓙ
31 Ⓐ Ⓑ Ⓒ Ⓓ
32 Ⓕ Ⓖ Ⓗ Ⓙ
33 Ⓐ Ⓑ Ⓒ Ⓓ
34 Ⓕ Ⓖ Ⓗ Ⓙ

35 Ⓐ Ⓑ Ⓒ Ⓓ
36 Ⓕ Ⓖ Ⓗ Ⓙ
37 Ⓐ Ⓑ Ⓒ Ⓓ
38 Ⓕ Ⓖ Ⓗ Ⓙ

# Answer Sheet

**STUDENT'S NAME**

| LAST | | FIRST | MI |
|------|--|-------|-----|

**SCHOOL:**

**TEACHER:**

FEMALE ○     MALE ○

## BIRTH DATE

| MONTH | DAY | YEAR |
|-------|-----|------|
| Jan ○ | ⓪ ⓪ | ⓪ ⓪ |
| Feb ○ | ① ① | ① ① |
| Mar ○ | ② ② | ② ② |
| Apr ○ | ③ ③ | ③ ③ |
| May ○ | ④ | ④ ④ |
| Jun ○ | ⑤ | ⑤ ⑤ |
| Jul ○ | ⑥ | ⑥ ⑥ |
| Aug ○ | ⑦ | ⑦ ⑦ |
| Sep ○ | ⑧ | ⑧ ⑧ |
| Oct ○ | ⑨ | ⑨ ⑨ |
| Nov ○ | | |
| Dec ○ | | |

**GRADE** ④ ⑤ ⑥ ⑦ ⑧

## Core Skills: Test Preparation
# Grade 4
© Steck-Vaughn Company

---

### TEST 1     Reading Comprehension

SA Ⓐ Ⓑ Ⓒ Ⓓ
1 Ⓐ Ⓑ Ⓒ Ⓓ
2 Ⓕ Ⓖ Ⓗ Ⓙ
3 Ⓐ Ⓑ Ⓒ Ⓓ
4 Ⓕ Ⓖ Ⓗ Ⓙ
5 Ⓐ Ⓑ Ⓒ Ⓓ
6 OPEN ENDED
7 Ⓕ Ⓖ Ⓗ Ⓙ

8 Ⓐ Ⓑ Ⓒ Ⓓ
9 Ⓕ Ⓖ Ⓗ Ⓙ
10 Ⓐ Ⓑ Ⓒ Ⓓ
11 Ⓕ Ⓖ Ⓗ Ⓙ
12 OPEN ENDED
13 Ⓐ Ⓑ Ⓒ Ⓓ
14 Ⓕ Ⓖ Ⓗ Ⓙ
15 Ⓐ Ⓑ Ⓒ Ⓓ

16 Ⓕ Ⓖ Ⓗ Ⓙ
17 Ⓐ Ⓑ Ⓒ Ⓓ
18 Ⓕ Ⓖ Ⓗ Ⓙ
19 Ⓐ Ⓑ Ⓒ Ⓓ
20 Ⓕ Ⓖ Ⓗ Ⓙ
21 Ⓐ Ⓑ Ⓒ Ⓓ
22 Ⓕ Ⓖ Ⓗ Ⓙ
23 Ⓐ Ⓑ Ⓒ Ⓓ

24 Ⓕ Ⓖ Ⓗ Ⓙ
25 OPEN ENDED
26 Ⓐ Ⓑ Ⓒ Ⓓ
27 Ⓕ Ⓖ Ⓗ Ⓙ
28 Ⓐ Ⓑ Ⓒ Ⓓ
29 Ⓕ Ⓖ Ⓗ Ⓙ
30 Ⓐ Ⓑ Ⓒ Ⓓ
31 Ⓕ Ⓖ Ⓗ Ⓙ

32 OPEN ENDED
33 Ⓐ Ⓑ Ⓒ Ⓓ
34 Ⓕ Ⓖ Ⓗ Ⓙ
35 Ⓐ Ⓑ Ⓒ Ⓓ
36 Ⓕ Ⓖ Ⓗ Ⓙ
37 Ⓐ Ⓑ Ⓒ Ⓓ
38 Ⓕ Ⓖ Ⓗ Ⓙ
39 Ⓐ Ⓑ Ⓒ Ⓓ

40 Ⓕ Ⓖ Ⓗ Ⓙ
41 OPEN ENDED
42 Ⓐ Ⓑ Ⓒ Ⓓ
43 Ⓕ Ⓖ Ⓗ Ⓙ
44 Ⓐ Ⓑ Ⓒ Ⓓ
45 Ⓕ Ⓖ Ⓗ Ⓙ
46 Ⓐ Ⓑ Ⓒ Ⓓ

### TEST 2     Reading Vocabulary

SA Ⓐ Ⓑ Ⓒ Ⓓ
1 Ⓐ Ⓑ Ⓒ Ⓓ
2 Ⓕ Ⓖ Ⓗ Ⓙ
3 Ⓐ Ⓑ Ⓒ Ⓓ
4 Ⓕ Ⓖ Ⓗ Ⓙ

5 Ⓐ Ⓑ Ⓒ Ⓓ
6 Ⓕ Ⓖ Ⓗ Ⓙ
7 Ⓐ Ⓑ Ⓒ Ⓓ
8 Ⓕ Ⓖ Ⓗ Ⓙ
9 Ⓐ Ⓑ Ⓒ Ⓓ

SB Ⓐ Ⓑ Ⓒ Ⓓ
10 Ⓕ Ⓖ Ⓗ Ⓙ
11 Ⓐ Ⓑ Ⓒ Ⓓ
12 Ⓕ Ⓖ Ⓗ Ⓙ
13 Ⓐ Ⓑ Ⓒ Ⓓ

14 Ⓕ Ⓖ Ⓗ Ⓙ
SC Ⓐ Ⓑ Ⓒ Ⓓ
15 Ⓐ Ⓑ Ⓒ Ⓓ
16 Ⓕ Ⓖ Ⓗ Ⓙ
17 Ⓐ Ⓑ Ⓒ Ⓓ

18 Ⓕ Ⓖ Ⓗ Ⓙ
19 Ⓐ Ⓑ Ⓒ Ⓓ
20 Ⓕ Ⓖ Ⓗ Ⓙ
21 Ⓐ Ⓑ Ⓒ Ⓓ
22 Ⓕ Ⓖ Ⓗ Ⓙ

## TEST 3    Part 1: Math Problem Solving

| | | | | |
|---|---|---|---|---|
| SA Ⓐ Ⓑ Ⓒ Ⓓ | 9 OPEN ENDED | 18 OPEN ENDED | 27 Ⓐ Ⓑ Ⓒ Ⓓ | 36 Ⓐ Ⓑ Ⓒ Ⓓ | 45 OPEN ENDED |
| 1 Ⓐ Ⓑ Ⓒ Ⓓ | 10 Ⓕ Ⓖ Ⓗ Ⓙ | 19 Ⓕ Ⓖ Ⓗ Ⓙ | 28 Ⓕ Ⓖ Ⓗ Ⓙ | 37 Ⓕ Ⓖ Ⓗ Ⓙ | 46 Ⓐ Ⓑ Ⓒ Ⓓ |
| 2 Ⓕ Ⓖ Ⓗ Ⓙ | 11 Ⓐ Ⓑ Ⓒ Ⓓ | 20 Ⓐ Ⓑ Ⓒ Ⓓ | 29 Ⓐ Ⓑ Ⓒ Ⓓ | 38 Ⓐ Ⓑ Ⓒ Ⓓ | 47 Ⓕ Ⓖ Ⓗ Ⓙ |
| 3 Ⓐ Ⓑ Ⓒ Ⓓ | 12 Ⓕ Ⓖ Ⓗ Ⓙ | 21 OPEN ENDED | 30 Ⓕ Ⓖ Ⓗ Ⓙ | 39 Ⓕ Ⓖ Ⓗ Ⓙ | 48 Ⓐ Ⓑ Ⓒ Ⓓ |
| 4 Ⓕ Ⓖ Ⓗ Ⓙ | 13 Ⓐ Ⓑ Ⓒ Ⓓ | 22 Ⓕ Ⓖ Ⓗ Ⓙ | 31 Ⓐ Ⓑ Ⓒ Ⓓ | 40 Ⓐ Ⓑ Ⓒ Ⓓ | 49 Ⓕ Ⓖ Ⓗ Ⓙ |
| 5 Ⓐ Ⓑ Ⓒ Ⓓ | 14 Ⓕ Ⓖ Ⓗ Ⓙ | 23 Ⓐ Ⓑ Ⓒ Ⓓ | 32 OPEN ENDED | 41 Ⓕ Ⓖ Ⓗ Ⓙ | |
| 6 Ⓕ Ⓖ Ⓗ Ⓙ | 15 Ⓐ Ⓑ Ⓒ Ⓓ | 24 Ⓕ Ⓖ Ⓗ Ⓙ | 33 Ⓕ Ⓖ Ⓗ Ⓙ | 42 OPEN ENDED | |
| 7 Ⓐ Ⓑ Ⓒ Ⓓ | 16 Ⓕ Ⓖ Ⓗ Ⓙ | 25 Ⓐ Ⓑ Ⓒ Ⓓ | 34 Ⓐ Ⓑ Ⓒ Ⓓ | 43 Ⓐ Ⓑ Ⓒ Ⓓ | |
| 8 OPEN ENDED | 17 Ⓐ Ⓑ Ⓒ Ⓓ | 26 Ⓕ Ⓖ Ⓗ Ⓙ | 35 Ⓕ Ⓖ Ⓗ Ⓙ | 44 Ⓕ Ⓖ Ⓗ Ⓙ | |

### Part 2: Math Procedures

| | | | | | |
|---|---|---|---|---|---|
| SA Ⓐ Ⓑ Ⓒ Ⓓ Ⓔ | 3 Ⓐ Ⓑ Ⓒ Ⓓ Ⓔ | 6 Ⓕ Ⓖ Ⓗ Ⓙ Ⓚ | 9 Ⓕ Ⓖ Ⓗ Ⓙ Ⓚ | 11 Ⓕ Ⓖ Ⓗ Ⓙ Ⓚ | 14 Ⓕ Ⓖ Ⓗ Ⓙ Ⓚ |
| 1 Ⓐ Ⓑ Ⓒ Ⓓ Ⓔ | 4 Ⓕ Ⓖ Ⓗ Ⓙ Ⓚ | 7 Ⓐ Ⓑ Ⓒ Ⓓ Ⓔ | SB Ⓐ Ⓑ Ⓒ Ⓓ Ⓔ | 12 OPEN ENDED | 15 Ⓐ Ⓑ Ⓒ Ⓓ Ⓔ |
| 2 Ⓕ Ⓖ Ⓗ Ⓙ Ⓚ | 5 Ⓐ Ⓑ Ⓒ Ⓓ Ⓔ | 8 OPEN ENDED | 10 Ⓐ Ⓑ Ⓒ Ⓓ Ⓔ | 13 Ⓐ Ⓑ Ⓒ Ⓓ Ⓔ | |

## TEST 4    Listening

| | | | | | |
|---|---|---|---|---|---|
| SA Ⓐ Ⓑ Ⓒ Ⓓ | 5 Ⓐ Ⓑ Ⓒ Ⓓ | 10 Ⓕ Ⓖ Ⓗ Ⓙ | 14 Ⓕ Ⓖ Ⓗ Ⓙ | 19 Ⓐ Ⓑ Ⓒ Ⓓ | 24 Ⓕ Ⓖ Ⓗ Ⓙ |
| 1 Ⓐ Ⓑ Ⓒ Ⓓ | 6 Ⓕ Ⓖ Ⓗ Ⓙ | 11 Ⓐ Ⓑ Ⓒ Ⓓ | 15 Ⓐ Ⓑ Ⓒ Ⓓ | 20 Ⓕ Ⓖ Ⓗ Ⓙ | 25 Ⓐ Ⓑ Ⓒ Ⓓ |
| 2 Ⓕ Ⓖ Ⓗ Ⓙ | 7 Ⓐ Ⓑ Ⓒ Ⓓ | 12 Ⓕ Ⓖ Ⓗ Ⓙ | 16 Ⓕ Ⓖ Ⓗ Ⓙ | 21 Ⓐ Ⓑ Ⓒ Ⓓ | |
| 3 Ⓐ Ⓑ Ⓒ Ⓓ | 8 Ⓕ Ⓖ Ⓗ Ⓙ | 13 Ⓐ Ⓑ Ⓒ Ⓓ | 17 Ⓐ Ⓑ Ⓒ Ⓓ | 22 Ⓕ Ⓖ Ⓗ Ⓙ | |
| 4 Ⓕ Ⓖ Ⓗ Ⓙ | 9 Ⓐ Ⓑ Ⓒ Ⓓ | SB Ⓐ Ⓑ Ⓒ Ⓓ | 18 Ⓕ Ⓖ Ⓗ Ⓙ | 23 Ⓐ Ⓑ Ⓒ Ⓓ | |

## TEST 5    Language

| | | | | | |
|---|---|---|---|---|---|
| SA Ⓐ Ⓑ Ⓒ Ⓓ | 7 Ⓐ Ⓑ Ⓒ Ⓓ | 14 Ⓕ Ⓖ Ⓗ Ⓙ | 21 Ⓐ Ⓑ Ⓒ Ⓓ | 28 Ⓕ Ⓖ Ⓗ Ⓙ | 35 Ⓐ Ⓑ Ⓒ Ⓓ |
| 1 Ⓐ Ⓑ Ⓒ Ⓓ | 8 OPEN ENDED | 15 Ⓐ Ⓑ Ⓒ Ⓓ | 22 Ⓕ Ⓖ Ⓗ Ⓙ | 29 Ⓐ Ⓑ Ⓒ Ⓓ | 36 Ⓕ Ⓖ Ⓗ Ⓙ |
| 2 Ⓕ Ⓖ Ⓗ Ⓙ | 9 Ⓕ Ⓖ Ⓗ Ⓙ | 16 Ⓕ Ⓖ Ⓗ Ⓙ | 23 Ⓐ Ⓑ Ⓒ Ⓓ | 30 Ⓕ Ⓖ Ⓗ Ⓙ | 37 Ⓐ Ⓑ Ⓒ Ⓓ |
| 3 Ⓐ Ⓑ Ⓒ Ⓓ | 10 Ⓐ Ⓑ Ⓒ Ⓓ | 17 Ⓐ Ⓑ Ⓒ Ⓓ | 24 Ⓕ Ⓖ Ⓗ Ⓙ | 31 Ⓐ Ⓑ Ⓒ Ⓓ | 38 Ⓕ Ⓖ Ⓗ Ⓙ |
| 4 Ⓕ Ⓖ Ⓗ Ⓙ | 11 Ⓕ Ⓖ Ⓗ Ⓙ | 18 Ⓕ Ⓖ Ⓗ Ⓙ | 25 Ⓐ Ⓑ Ⓒ Ⓓ | 32 Ⓕ Ⓖ Ⓗ Ⓙ | |
| 5 Ⓐ Ⓑ Ⓒ Ⓓ | 12 OPEN ENDED | 19 Ⓐ Ⓑ Ⓒ Ⓓ | 26 Ⓕ Ⓖ Ⓗ Ⓙ | 33 Ⓐ Ⓑ Ⓒ Ⓓ | |
| 6 Ⓕ Ⓖ Ⓗ Ⓙ | 13 Ⓐ Ⓑ Ⓒ Ⓓ | 20 Ⓕ Ⓖ Ⓗ Ⓙ | 27 Ⓐ Ⓑ Ⓒ Ⓓ | 34 Ⓕ Ⓖ Ⓗ Ⓙ | |